MAKE MONEY WITH FACEBOOK ADVERTISING

Learn How to Make $300+ Per Day Online With Facebook Marketing and Make Passive Income in Less Than 24 Hours

By
James Ericson

TABLE OF CONTENTS

INTRODUCTION

Congratulations on taking the first steps toward mastering Facebook advertising and boosting your profits!

Social media represents an unprecedented opportunity for business. The problem is, most business owners don't know how to utilize it. And that's a shame because advertising and marketing on social media can help grow your business and find new customers rapidly.

In this book, we're going to teach you how to use Facebook to laser target prospects that you can turn into buying customers or high paying clients. If you're a noob now, by the time you finish this book, you'll understand how to utilize Facebook to make your business explode within 24 hours – at low cost.

We'll explore:

- What is Social Media Marketing? In this chapter, we'll review the various social media marketing outlets, and discuss what makes social media different from traditional media.
- Why Facebook Advertising. This chapter introduces you to an overview of Facebook advertising, giving you a taste as to why Facebook is head and shoulders above the rest when it comes to a powerful marketing platform.
- Getting started on Facebook. In this chapter, we will learn how to create a Facebook Page and then work on our first Facebook Ad campaign.
- Targeting Customers. In this chapter, we will go into detail on the different ways that you can target Facebook users.
- Audience Insights. Next, we explore a powerful tool that is built into Facebook that lets you research your ad demographics. This includes basic things like age and gender but also drills down into page likes and more that will help you understand your customers.

- Facebook Pixel. What is Facebook Pixel? Find out in this chapter and learn how you can use it to collect data on people that visit and use your website.
- Introduction to Facebook Ads Manager. In this chapter, we go into more detail on the Facebook Ads Manager.
- Analyzing Results. Proper analysis of the results of your campaigns will help you determine which ones to keep, which ones need refinement, and which ones to trash.
- Traffic vs. Page Likes. In this chapter, we help you understand the differences between these two campaigns that can drive traffic to your business.
- Lookalike Audiences. Perhaps the most powerful tool in internet marketing. Learn what they are, how to use them, and how to profit from them.
- Creative Media Types. In this chapter, we'll go into detail to learn the various creative types that you can use in your advertisements.
- Boosted and Promoted Posts. Learn how to advertise specific postings from your Facebook page.
- Common Mistakes Made by Newbies. We go over common mistakes made by beginners that we've identified.
- Facebook Business Manager. Learn about the Facebook Business Manager and how it can help with the administrative tasks related to Facebook advertising.

By the time you finish this book, you will have a solid handle on the fundamental principles behind Facebook advertising and what it takes to use it to grow your business and take it to the next level.

There are many books on Facebook advertising on the market. We'd like to thank you for choosing this one and we sincerely hope that you will find it informative and that you'll gain some actionable tips from it!

CHAPTER 1
What Is Social Media Marketing?

Everywhere you turn, these days you're hearing about social media. Whether it's the President or some Hollywood star tweeting, or the latest news about Facebook, it seems like everyone is on it and everyone is obsessing over it.

Why is marketing on social media important? And in particular, why is it important for business?

Let's look at some of the reasons:

- Everyone is on social media, and they're spending more time on it.
- It's become the primary way to communicate with friends or family, especially about products or the news.
- Social media actually allows you to incorporate multiple types of *creative* media into one or more posts. By this, we mean incorporating text, video, and audio together, or using them separately.
- Unlike television or radio, social media can give you global exposure – or you can fine tune to the most local exposure imaginable.
- It works for any interest or type of business – from promoting video games to beauty shops to real estate.
- It's easy to find customers who already want your product or service.

Social media can even be exploited for free by business, but the reality of that is it takes time. If you want to use social media for free then you'd have to spend months and months – maybe more than a year – working hours each day to build up an audience. We're not going to say that can't work, but chances are you're looking to build your business and find new prospects *today*. The good news is that it's entirely possible because you can start running ads on multiple platforms and do it instantly – at very low cost.

While running ads on television or radio on a local basis could cost you thousands or tens of thousands of dollars, advertising on social media can cost you as little as $3 a day. On a per prospect basis, you can acquire prospects for a few cents.

Of course, that is if you know the tricks of the trade.

But it doesn't end there. Using traditional media, if you want to go national, it would literally require an advertising and marketing budget in the millions of dollars. And then trying to advertise worldwide? *Forget about it.*

Not so with social media.

With social media, not only can you easily target any and all locations in the United States, you can advertise *anywhere* on planet earth. OK let's say virtually anywhere, there might be one or two exceptions. But if Facebook, YouTube or Twitter is operating in that country – you can advertise there.

And the good thing is that the prices will be the same or cheaper.

Just think about that for a moment – a few decades ago to run a nationwide TV ad you had to spend millions. You had to hire a fancy ad agency to make the video for you and edit it. Then you had to arrange for placements with major TV or cable networks that would cost millions for a 30-second ad.

Fast forward to today, and you can make your own video on your computer in a couple of hours, and then run it worldwide for a few dollars.

Stunning isn't it?

Well, maybe your business isn't looking for global customers. You might be an attorney or a real estate agent looking for local folks in your proximity. The good news is that social media works like gangbusters for you too! As we'll see, you can laser target prospects at dirt cheap prices, making it easy as could be to get new, paying customers.

Now even though we are talking about paid advertising, the ubiquitous sharing and interactive features of social media will play a big role in your campaigns. That is huge, and something entirely new for business. Sure, in the old days someone could see a commercial or product they liked and they might mention it to their friends. But the reach was limited and mentioning a funny commercial to someone you know is hardly the same as actually letting them *see* it for themselves. Today, you can post an advertisement on social media – and people who find it useful, funny, or enjoyable can share it with their friends. And then they share it with their friends...and pretty soon it "goes viral" and get far more views than you actually paid for.

So what are all the major social media networks? You probably know them already, but just in case you don't let's review them

- Facebook: This is the biggie and the topic of this book. Facebook essentially launched the social media revolution. Even though Facebook wasn't the first (remember MySpace?), Facebook turned social media from a side curiosity for young people into a *must-have* tool that connects friends, family, and people that shared interests or hobbies. Worldwide, not everyone is on Facebook, but globally Facebook has 2.32 *billion* monthly active users. Every day, 1.52 billion people log into Facebook at least once.
- Twitter: Twitter has enabled people to communicate with the public on an instant and unprecedented scale. Twitter is smaller and more concentrated in the United States, Canada, Europe, and Australia, but with 321 million users in 2019, it still has a major impact. News organizations constantly monitor Twitter and use them in articles to share opinions. You'd be surprised, while they mostly focus on public figures, when a post by an unknown person goes viral it can show up on leading news publications too.
- YouTube: YouTube, the video engine, has 1.3 billion users. It's estimated that 5 billion videos are watched on YouTube every single day and that 300 hours of video footage are uploaded to the site every minute. In our estimation, YouTube ranks second only to Facebook as a platform to reach customers (and in the English speaking countries, it's

probably on equal footing), and you can use YouTube and Facebook in conjunction with each other to extend your reach.

- Instagram: This company is based on image sharing and it sprung to life as a result of the incorporation of cameras into smartphones. As soon as people were able to take pictures anywhere and anytime, they wanted to share them with the world. The good news for you is that Instagram was acquired by Facebook and so you can advertise on both simultaneously.
- Pinterest: Another image sharing site.
- Stumble Upon: A site that can be used to share articles.
- Gab: A lesser known message site that works like Twitter.
- Vimeo: Another video uploading site.
- Daily Motion: A video sharing website like YouTube.
- Linked In: The social network where people post their resumes and make professional connections. Growing in importance, but not the focus of this book.

In our opinion, while you can spend time going crazy trying to learn about and target every social media network out there, the only two you really need to worry about our Facebook and YouTube. Twitter is actually losing users. It was reported that between January 2018 and January 2019, it's active user base actually declined by 9 million, or about 2%. Secondly advertising on Twitter isn't as powerful as advertising on Facebook. It's harder to target by interest or make your ads as compelling to view. And since Facebook and YouTube are going to give you complete coverage of your audience, it's more productive to focus on those rather than trying to hit everything.

Hopefully, we've convinced you that social media marketing is a very useful tool for business. Now let's take a look at Facebook specifically.

CHAPTER 2
Why Facebook Advertising

We've gone over the stats – billions of people are using Facebook every month, and more than a billion are getting on it daily. In fact, a large fraction of people are getting on it multiple times a day. Whether people are on their desktop computer or out with their smartphone, little dings keep bringing Facebook messages posted by their friends to their attention – and drawing them back to the site.

Whether that's a good thing or not for society at large we'll leave to the experts. As business marketers – our only concern is getting our message out to where the people are, and doing it at the lowest possible cost. And Facebook is the ideal platform for that.

Let's have a look at some of the reasons why you would specifically want to use Facebook for your advertising campaigns.

Laser Targeting

Facebook lets you do an unprecedented amount of laser targeting of prospects. By being able to "zoom in" on who your prospects are, you can give yourself an automatic edge before your marketing campaigns even begin. In the old days, you had to make an advertisement for radio or television, and throw them out for the entire world to see. Maybe only 3% of the demo in your city is interested in your product or service, but there was no way to target them using rich media as a television ad. You had to spend money on targeting everyone. Now it was possible to target people with specific needs and interests by say using direct mail or advertising in magazines, but that kind of advertising isn't nearly as effective as having a video show up on their Facebook feed.

Let's look at some of the ways you can target Facebook users:

- Location: You can target by location as broadly or as targeted as you like. For example, you could run an advertisement that targets users in the United States,

Canada, Australia, New Zealand, and Great Britain. Or, you could target users within one mile of a specific street corner in Portland, Oregon.

- Interest: One of the things Facebook has done is catalog people's interests. Whether it's bowling, playing casino games on their iPhone, learning how to code software or invest in real estate, people build up a profile of their interests by liking pages and joining groups. Facebook lets you target ads by interests.
- Similar Products: Often, those page likes are for other products that might be similar to yours. Sell a basketball game for the iPhone? You can target people who've liked pages related to basketball and those who have downloaded other basketball games from the App Store. That's just one example – it works for any product or service.
- Age: Depending on your product or service, you can target people of any age from 13 and up.
- Gender: You can run ads targeted toward males, or females, or all.
- Employer: Some companies have a presence on Facebook, and you can target people who have indicated they work there.
- School: Some people have noted what university they attended, making it possible to do some targeting here.

Later, when we look at audience insights we will explore the ability to laser target your audience in more detail.

Lookalike Audiences

The *lookalike* audience is one of the most powerful features of Facebook advertising. The way this works is that you can get an audience of customers that have purchased some product or responded to an ad for a certain product. Then Facebook will analyze it to find out the characteristics of that group of people. We don't know how it works behind the scenes, but they do it. For example, if you are making an advertisement to sell bankruptcy services for your law office, you can have Facebook analyze an audience of people who have previously responded to advertisements for bankruptcy services, and then create a lookalike audience. You can then create an advertisement that targets that audience.

Why do that?

Because the lookalike audience is going to be super responsive – and so it's going to drive down the costs of acquiring new prospects.

So how do you get lookalike audiences? Well, they aren't free. You can either obtain them from someone else, or you can build them yourself. The fastest way is to either approach people with a prospect list or a broker and buy the list. It should have an email address and first and last name. Alternatively, you can build one yourself. The list should have at least 1,000 prospects but 5,000 is a very good number. The way you will build one yourself is to run ads basically cold until you've gotten 1,000+ people to respond to the ad. Then on your second run, you can build your ad around the lookalike audience that Facebook creates based on the prospects you gathered from the initial ad. The costs associated with your second ad will be much lower.

Think of lookalike audiences as cloning previous customers!

Facebook is Dirt Cheap

We've talked about the expenses of marketing with traditional media. They can run anywhere from a few bucks for a classified ad in a newspaper all the way up to millions of dollars for a TV spot. The great thing about Facebook is that you can advertise for dirt cheap! Of course, you have to know what you are doing. If you are spending $20 a day advertising and not getting results, you may as well gather a pile of cash and light it on fire. But luckily after you read this book you'll be armed with the knowledge you need to make ads that work at low cost.

You can literally start running ads on Facebook for as little as $2.50 per day.

We can see the benefits by looking at the cost to reach 1,000 people using different types of media:

9

- Newspaper: $32
- Magazine: $20
- Radio: $8
- Cable TV: $7
- Google Adwords: $2.75
- Facebook: $0.25

Now, the thing is – you can't approach a radio station and say "I'd like to run an advertisement that will reach 1,000 people. Here is my check for $8". If you run an ad on the radio – you must target the entire audience. Which is one reason that the traditional methods of advertising are so expensive?

Of course, costs are going to vary. Every time that you launch a Facebook advertising campaign, it's not going to come in at the $0.25 cents per 1,000 people range. But there is no doubt that it's going to be cheaper than traditional advertising methods and even Google Adwords, which quite frankly has grown a lot more expensive over the years. Also while you can't control the number of people reached using Radio or TV, with Facebook that's actually something that you'll be able to tune.

You are in Control

Facebook ads are under your direct control at all times. You can turn them on and off at will, so run ads when it's most relevant. You can also kill campaigns that don't work quickly. Imagine if you had spent $10,000 on a magazine ad in the old days. You'd probably have to wait 2-3 months before it even ran. Then you'd have to sit back and see how it worked out. If the ad was a dud, you were out of luck.

With Facebook, you can run an advertisement for a day, and then kill it if it didn't generate any prospects. Then you can make adjustments and have a new ad up in running in a few minutes. With that magazine ad, you'd have to make tweaks and wait another 2 months – while spending another $10,000. In today's fast-paced electronic world that kind of delay would be fatal to a new business.

Global Reach

Earlier we mentioned that you can use Facebook for laser targeting. So maybe you only want to advertise to people that live in the Orange County region near Los Angeles. You can do that with Facebook. But if instead, you want to advertise to people in North America, Europe, and China, you can do that too. Or you can even run ads worldwide. Whatever you choose, Facebook makes it easy.

Even better, it's very easy to target ads by location. If you need to, you can have specific ad creatives that are targeted to each of your primary geos. Try and imagine how many millions of dollars it would cost to run a global television advertising campaign. On Facebook, you reach a worldwide audience for a few dollars a day and a few clicks of the mouse.

Your Customers are on Facebook

OK, we won't keep harping on this – but more than two billion people are on Facebook. In the United States and Canada, it's fair to say *everyone* is on Facebook. It doesn't matter what product or service you sell – your customers *are* on Facebook. This isn't even debatable. Even if you are targeting seniors – while the share of the demo on Facebook will be lower – there are still large numbers of them using Facebook that you can reach.

Retargeting and Return Visitors

One thing that Facebook lets you do is advertise to people that have visited your site but not converted into customers. If they visited the site they do have some interest. You can warm them into buyers at low cost using Facebook advertising.

The Power of the Pixel

The Facebook Pixel might be second only to lookalike audiences when it comes to powerful advertising tools. The Pixel is a bit of code that you can add to your web pages that will track what your users are doing. Imagine being able to assemble a database of users who visited your website, added something to a shopping cart, and then left the site without actually placing an order. Then since everything is integrated, you can run a quick Facebook ad campaign to bring them back to your site to complete the order. Of course, it's not going to work with everyone, but it's going to boost your sales, that much we can say for sure.

If you don't have your own personally managed website and are using a third party tool like Drupal, Wix, or Wordpress, the good news is that Facebook has you covered here too. These companies have become partners of Facebook and installation of the pixel can be done practically automatically. It even works with Shopify.

If working with code seems too complicated for you, Facebook makes it easy to get the code to a developer that you specify so that they can integrate it into your website for you.

Media Creatives

You can target Facebook users with video, slideshows, single images, or carousels that mix video and images together. Multiple creative types mean more ways to create ads and do A/B testing to find out what really works with your customer base. If you don't have your own images, Facebook provides stock images that you can use in ads. Slide shows are a low tech way to up the game for your single image creatives, and carousels allow you to mix various single image and video creatives together into a single ad. They also have a "video creation kit". If you don't have a video available, you can upload or select still images that Facebook will use to create a video with some special effects that make it look professionally produced.

Interactivity

Facebook ads operate like regular posts. So the viewer can comment, like the post, share it, or post a reaction. The ability to have an interaction with the ad is a major advantage – and obviously not something you could do with a TV, radio or magazine ad. You can even respond to comments people leave if you like and you might find people who are commenting getting into their own discussions. Imagine having the ability to directly answer a question someone leaves on your advertisement, in near real time.

Customer Feedback

To run ads on Facebook, you will need to have a Facebook page. This will provide you with a free customer center that you can use to communicate directly with prospects as if you were their Facebook friend. It will also give you a ready to use site where customers can give you feedback or file complaints and request help. You can also speak directly to your customers when doing research, asking them to offer their opinions on changes you're going to make or new products you're thinking about bringing to market. Keep it active and keep it engaged.

Sharing

We just mentioned that people can share your ad – so if you have a good ad it could even "go viral". That can mean a whole lot of eyeballs on your advertisements free of charge. Even if it doesn't, some people are going to share your ad which means your ad will get in front of more people – and the customers are doing the work for you.

Well, that does it for our list of reasons you should advertise on Facebook. Hopefully, you're convinced! There are probably many more reasons but we think these are sufficient.

CHAPTER 3
Getting Started On Facebook

In this chapter, we'll learn about some basics you need to set up in order to take full advantage of the Facebook advertising platform. We'll begin by looking at Facebook pages, basic ad setup, types of campaigns, and budgeting.

Facebook Pages

A Facebook page is basically a web page that you set up on Facebook. It's free to set up and provides a platform you can use to "share" information. Like everything else on Facebook, it has a stream where you can add posts. It also has an About page and you can upload photos and buttons. The buttons can be used to set up interactivity with your users, such as prompting them to sign-up for an email list. In short, a Facebook page is like another Facebook profile, but for your business.

In order to set up a Facebook page, you need to have a Facebook profile for yourself. Don't worry though, Facebook keeps the pages you create separation from your personal profile. None of your friends and family will see the Facebook page unless you invite them to it. You may, or may not, want to invite your Facebook friends to like the page. That will depend on your specific situation and the product or service you're offering. Conversely, visitors to your page can't link it back to your personal profile, unless you want to explicitly reveal that information.

A Facebook page is required to run advertisements on Facebook. As we'll see, when you create a Facebook ad it's going to ask you which Facebook page you're linking the ad too. You can have one or multiple Facebook pages, and they can all be for different products, businesses, or personalities. The personalities can be "pen names" if that suits your purpose.

Besides being required to launch a Facebook ad, a Facebook page provides many advantages on its own. When someone likes your Facebook page, it shows up on their feed. So friends and family will see that the person has liked the page, and those who have similar interests might decide to visit your page as well.

Moreover, once someone has liked your page, it's as if your business has become a "friend" on Facebook. Think about how Facebook operates. When someone becomes your "friend", every time they post something on Facebook it shows up on your feed. If you have the mobile app with notifications turned on, these posts will ding your phone and show up like text message alerts on your screen.

A Facebook page operates in the same way. Every time you post on a Facebook page, the post will show up in the feeds of people who have liked the page. Relevant content will draw eyeballs from their friends, who may be drawn to like your page or to share it with others. This can start a snowball effect that could become viral, but at the very least will give you extra exposure even if it doesn't become one of the world's most popular postings.

Facebook pages can be used in conjunction not only with advertisements but to establish a wide internet presence. We suggest that you also set up two other avenues where you can post content and link them all together:

- Start a blog
- Start a YouTube channel

This provides a way to start backlinking and widening your presence online. For example, the following technique will be very helpful for promoting your business without spending extra money.

- Write a blog post
- Post the blog article to your Facebook page

An even better approach would be:

- Create a short video relevant to some problems your product or service solves.
- Post it on YouTube. In the video description, place a link to your Facebook page, and a link to your blog.

- Now write an article on your blog about the topic. It can be very short, but be sure to include your YouTube video in the post, with a link at the end of your article to the video.
- Then go to your Facebook page, and create new post linking to your blog article.

These techniques will help boost your blog and YouTube channels, and vice versa – attracting more traffic to your Facebook page. Backlinking will help drive some organic traffic over time.

We suggest doing this at least three times per week. The more you post, the more traffic you're going to get over time, but if you are focusing on paid Facebook traffic then you don't need to break your back using organic methods. The key to building and keeping a good customer base, however, is continually providing them with some useful content. This also helps build trust in the marketplace and establishes you as an authority figure in your niche, which will help make your advertising campaigns more successful.

A central approach to making this work is knowing what keywords to target. Jump on Google and search for "Google Keyword Planner". You can use this tool to find keywords that people are searching for related to your business. Then you can build a series of articles based on the keyword.

Let's suppose that we are an attorney offering bankruptcy services. Looking at Google Keyword Planner, we can identify several relevant keywords/phrases that we can use to write blog posts, make short videos about, and post both to our Facebook page:

- Filing bankruptcy chapter 7
- Bankruptcy attorney
- Bankruptcy lawyer
- Debt consolidation programs
- How to get out of debt
- When to declare bankruptcy
- Filing chapter 13
- Bankruptcy attorney near me
- Bankruptcy information

And on and on. For each phrase, you should use the phrase in the title, two or three times in the article (or in the case of YouTube, the video description), and in the tags on the blog post and YouTube video. After you've posted your video and/or blog post to your Facebook page, you can also post related content from others on your Facebook page, and use that as an excuse to link back to your article.

Prepping for Running Ads

What you don't want to do, is have users show up at your Facebook page when you start running ads and have nothing on it. Even if you're starting from scratch, you want it to look like there is an established online presence. With that in mind, you should aim to put at least ten posts on your Facebook page before you run the first advertisement that is uniquely yours. Don't start posting content from others until you've started building up a base of people who have liked your page. It's better if you keep your content original rather than posting other people's content. And while outsourcing is a possibility, it's also a risk. At least, in the beginning, you want to be the one posting on the Facebook page so it will sound more genuine and also not like someone who speaks English as a second language wrote a post based on researching Wikipedia.

Aside: Starting a Blog

By far the easiest way to start a blog is to register with wordpress.com. You can take the free route or get a domain name. The point of the blog isn't to make money, its to provide substantial uniquely created content to add to your Facebook page. It's very easy to use and you don't have to bother with installing WordPress on a website. If you don't want to use wordpress.com, you can get a website on BlueHost or GoDaddy and then install Wordpress there fairly easily, but you might have to pay for a decent looking theme for the blog if you go that route.

Outsourcing Content

Some readers will be comfortable making their own content. But if you aren't or simply don't have time, you can outsource content creation at a low cost. The main site to use for this is Fiverr. You can find people who will write articles or make videos for you for a few bucks. Also, if you're not a good speaker on camera, Fiverr has plenty of voice professionals that you can hire for low prices. They can just read a script for you and put it in an audio file that can be overlaid on a video in a program like iMovie.

For video or written content, you can simply provide a sketch of what you want to be included in the content and tell them what keywords you are targeting. Many are SEO experts so will know how to write your articles so that they are well on search engines and get some organic traffic.

How to Create Your Facebook Page

Now let's go through the steps required to create the Facebook page. You're going to need two images, one for a profile picture and one for the "cover photo" which appears at the top of the page.

- Open up Facebook.com.
- On the left side, look for *Explore*.
- Click on *Pages*.
- This will open a new page showing pages you've liked.
- In the upper right, click on the *Create Page*.
- There are two choices, *Business or Brand* and *Community or Public Figure*.
- Choose the page type most appropriate for your situation – for authors, the public figure might be more appropriate for example.
- If you select Business or Brand, you'll be asked to name the page. You'll probably want to think of a name for your page ahead of time.
- You will also be asked to select a category. Start typing and a drop-down list will open. Select the category that most closely fits your business.
- If prompted enter information like your address. You can elect to hide the address from being displayed on the page.
- Next, upload a profile picture. A 200 x 200 px size image is good.
- Finally, you'll be asked for the cover photo. The exact dimensions aren't important but it should be about 2.6

times as wide as high, and at least 820 pixels wide. The exact size displayed on desktop computers is 820 x 312. Keep in mind that the cover photo is displayed as 640 x 320 on smartphones, so you might want the most relevant content in the middle of the image.

Once you complete these steps, your page is now up and running and you're reading to post. Be sure to bookmark it so you can access it quickly. Once it's up and running, you can edit the About page and start making posts. It works exactly like the Facebook you're used to so this is easy to manage. You can even post job openings here, and create an ad directly from the page.

How to Create Your First Ad

Now let's create our first ad. Since you've just created a Facebook page, one of the first ads you'll want to run on Facebook is a page likes campaign. We want to start building a fan base for our business. So before you go forward to this step, follow our previous advice and put at least ten postings on your Facebook page with relevant content related to your product or service. When we run our ad, we want people to see a page that has relevant content.

To create ads, you will go to the Ads Manager page:

https://business.facebook.com/adsmanager/

The page will have a list of campaigns you've created (obviously blank the first time you visit the page) along with the following tabs:

- Account Overview
- Opportunities
- Campaigns
- Ad sets for one campaign
- Ads for 1 campaign

The levels of the tree are a little bit confusing to new users, we will discuss these in more detail in the chapter on the Ads Manager. For now, draw your attention to the green *Create* button on the left side of the screen. This is what we use to create new campaigns.

When you click Create, You will see three broad categories:

- Awareness
- Consideration
- Conversion

Under Awareness, the options are:

- Brand Awareness
- Reach

For Consideration, we have:

- Traffic
- Engagement
- App Installs
- Video Views
- Lead Generation
- Messages

Finally, under Conversion we have:

- Conversions
- Catalog Sales
- Store Traffic

Seeing all these choices, it can be daunting to know what kind of campaign you need to run (unless you have a mobile app business, and are running an App Installs campaign). Here are some basic rules.

Traffic is simply a campaign that directs people who see your advertisement to a specific website. In particular, you use traffic to drive traffic *outside* of Facebook.

If you have a Shopify store or are selling on Amazon, then your most relevant advertisements might be:

- Catalog Sales
- Store Traffic

If you have a brand you just want to make people aware of – maybe you sell barbecue sauce that's for sale in the grocery store, then brand awareness or reach might be the type of campaign that you should run.

If you're looking to build an email list of prospects, then Lead Generation or Traffic will work for you.

For our purposes right now, *Engagement*, which is located under *Consideration*, is the type of campaign we want to use. An Engagement campaign can be used for the following three purposes:

- Post Engagement: If you're interested in driving traffic to a specific post you've made on Facebook, then this is the option you should select.
- Page Likes: This is the type of campaign we will use in this example. It will get people engaged with the Facebook page you created and hopefully, garner a large number of page likes so that you'll be connected on Facebook with your prospects.
- Finally, there are events.

Click on the Page Likes button that you see on your screen in the middle. Now edit the Campaign Name field to give it a meaningful name. The default is engagement, we can change it to something like "Pagename(that you created) Page Likes".

If you want to create an A/B test – you can turn this switch on. But we'll leave it off for now. Finally, you can create multiple ad sets within a campaign. Each ad set has its own budget settings, but you can turn to Optimize budget across ad sets to spread the budget across the multiple ad sets (if you create more than one) and have it optimize the spending.

Frankly, I prefer to do things manually, in the sense of setting up individual campaigns and test them against each other rather than using the built-in A/B testing and optimization. Doing it manually is actually pretty simple, and you can turn off and delete campaigns that don't work.

So we'll select Page Likes and click on *Continue* at the bottom of the page. The next page that opens on our screen is where we select the page that we want to advertise, you will see this at the very top where it says Page☐Facebook Page☐Select Page. Just click open the drop-down list and you'll see the page you created there.

Next, we will see the *Audience* section. We aren't going to worry about this right now until we've reviewed *Audience Insights*. But you can create an audience of targeted prospects here, or used a previously saved audience. However, as we'll see in a minute, even without selecting an audience or having one ready, we can laser target our prospects.

The next section is your Locations. If you click to open the drop-down list, it gives you the following options:

- Everyone in this location
- People who live in this location (the default)
- People recently in this location
- People traveling in this location

The last option is a really interesting one – great to use if you have a tourist related business. For example, if you have a bed and breakfast, you could run advertisements in your area targeting people who are traveling.

Next, it has a default location setup. If you are in the United States, that is what it will have there (and ditto for your country if you live outside the United States). If desired, you can add multiple countries to the list. Simply click on *Include* and start typing the name of the country, city, or state that you want to include. You can also exclude locations using this entry.

If you want to zoom in on a precise location and advertise within a certain radius, use this method. When you click on the Include input box, you will notice that a map appears below it. You can pan around the map and click the + button to zoom in. Then, click *drop pin* once with your mouse, and click once on the location on the map you want. The default radius is 10 miles (or km). If you click that open, a slider bar will open that you can use to adjust the radius from the pin location where you want your advertisement to be displayed. The range is 1 to 50 miles.

If you've entered a location you decide you don't want, simply hover your mouse over the location in the list and click on the X button on the far right to delete it.

For our example, we entered California for our location, so the add will target people who live in California.

Next, we find general demographic information: Age, Gender, and Language. Select these as appropriate for your target audience. Keep in mind that you can have different advertisements for the same product or service that target males, or females, and/or different age groups.

The next section is *Detailed Targeting*. This is a very important section for your first advertisement. This is where you specify various interests or associations of people that are important or relevant to your product or service. Click the box where it says *Add demographics, interests, or behaviors*. Then simply start typing something relevant.

For example, if we want to target a specific demographic, say U.S. Latinos, you can type in *Hispanic*. You will see multiple options popup, including primary language spoken. For the sake of example, let's say we are a California bankruptcy attorney who wants to target English speaking Hispanics that are interested in getting bankruptcy assistance. First, we click on *Hispanic (U.S. – English dominant)*.

You can select as many special interests as you want. Generally, we recommend adding at least five, but it's good to add up to twenty. For our example, we select *Bankruptcy, Consumer Debt, Dave Ramsey*, and *Legal Services*. If you're not familiar with him, Dave Ramsey is a radio personality. We selected Dave Ramsey because he is a personal finance advisor, and people often call his show when they are massively in debt. By targeting people who've visited the Dave Ramsey Facebook page, we might find some prospects who are interested in hiring a bankruptcy attorney.

At the bottom, you have an option to save the audience. If you've made your selections and think you'll want to use them with other advertisements you create, it's a good idea to save the audience.

Next, we come to *Placements*. When you're just starting, we recommend using Automatic Placements. This also works well when you're experienced, because you'll want to test your ads on different placements and then after some testing, you can run the ads for a bit and see which placement's don't work. It's easy to remove them by unchecking the box.

To do that click on Edit Placements. The options you'll see are:

- Facebook
- Instagram
- Audience Network
- Messenger

Within each, there are several subcategories. For Facebook we have:

- Feeds
- Instant Articles
- In-stream videos
- Right column
- Suggested videos
- Marketplace
- Stories

Unless you see your ad is a complete dud on specific items, you'll want to take all placements you're eligible for.

For Instagram, it's a different story. Some ads that work on Facebook won't work on Instagram. One reason is it's simply a platform with a different use, it's based on sharing images. Your product or service may or may not work there. Also, Instagram tends to be skewed toward a younger audience. If you are targeting people aged 18-29, then Instagram might be relevant. If you are targeting people 35+, it's probably not relevant. For Instagram, you can target feed or stories. Stories are short 10-15 second video clips, so an ad can be useful for stories – but that isn't as important as to whether or not your customer base is likely to be on Instagram. Also, people on Instagram probably aren't interested in seeing a video about bankruptcy on their stories, but someone on Facebook will be open to seeing it on their newsfeed. For our example, since we don't think bankruptcy attorney is a good topic to advertise for Instagram, we will deselect it, so that the impressions can be used for Facebook instead of wasting them on Instagram.

Next, we come to the Facebook audience network. This is an off-Facebook advertising option. It's an advertising network in mobile apps. If you are advertising a game or an app, then it's going to be relevant. It's not relevant for a lot of products and services, and can't be used for Page Likes – so we will deselect it.

Finally, you can have ads that show up in people's Facebook Messenger. However, this option isn't available for Page Likes, so we'll deselect it.

Scrolling down you will see that you can select options for mobile devices, operating systems, and whether or not someone is connected to WiFi. Generally, you can ignore these unless you have a mobile app that requires a certain version of iOS. If you have a product you want people to buy on the spot after looking at the ad, it's probably best to turn on the WiFi box. This will ensure that people are either at home or in a location where they are in a position to purchase, rather than running around just glancing at their phone.

Budgeting

Next, we come to the budget. Budget can be set as Daily, or for Lifetime. Usually, you will use the Daily. Facebook provides a suggested budget – however, we are going to ignore it. We'll see why later. For Page Likes, the suggested budget is $25. However, we're going to enter $5 for the daily budget. You can even start at $3.

The reason is that we are going to use the following approach:

- Test
- Scale-up

So for now, set a very low budget. We're going to run the ad and see what happens.

You can run the ad continuously (the default option) or specify that it runs for a specific date range. Either is fine, but don't worry about selecting run continuously, because you can turn ads on and off on the fly from the Ads Manager.

For Bid Strategy, you can use the Lowest Cost, or select a bid cap. For the Lowest Cost, Facebook will try to optimize your campaign. Sometimes this works, sometimes it doesn't. It depends on many factors including how well your audience is targeted. Bid cap can work sometimes as well. You specify the maximum you want to pay. Keep in mind this is not going to be something that works exactly – the system will try to find buyers that it can bid your ad to at that cost. Sometimes it will beat your bid cap but sometimes it will only come close. Also, bid cap campaigns can run pretty slowly compared to the Lowest Cost. It's hard to say ahead of time.

The best thing to do is try both – but for now, select the Lowest Cost. Later we will explain how you can duplicate a campaign. So you can create the Lowest Cost campaign, duplicate it, and then change the Bid Strategy in the copy to bid cap. However note that Facebook suggests a very high bid cap for page likes at $5. You could be getting your page likes for under a dollar. You don't have to take their suggestion, however. Set whatever bid cap you prefer and see how it works.

The last relevant item on this page is when you'll be charged – you can select impressions or per page like. Impressions are probably better but this is something you'll probably want to test in real time.

Finally, click continue so we can set the ad up and enter our creatives.

Next, you'll see *Format* where you can select one of the available options. These may vary depending on the campaign type that you've selected. Generally speaking, the options include:

- Single Image
- Slide show, or a set of images
- Video
- Carousel, where you can mix images and video together

Video is the most effective, but if you don't have a video an image only ad can still work pretty well. Facebook has also recently added some canned "videos" that you can create using image and text that are actually quite nice.

You can upload video and images from your computer, or you can use stock images supplied by Facebook. You have the options of creating six different ads using different images in your campaign.

Scrolling down, you'll have the chance to enter a text message and headline that will appear on the ad (headlines aren't used on Page Like campaigns, however, it displays the name of the page for the headline). You will also be able to preview the appearance of the ad for different placements.

If the ad is designed for traffic to an off-Facebook website, you'll be able to enter the URL of your web page here.

For different campaigns, you will also be able to select the message of the button displayed in the ad. For Page likes there is only a "thumbs up" and no button, but if you run a traffic ad you can select "Learn More" for example, or for app installs you can select "Play Game" or "Install Now". Each choice provides more options for testing to see what works best in your situation.

Finally, scroll down and select "Confirm". Once you do that, the waiting period begins.

What's Next

Facebook will review your ad campaign. Please note that lately because of some scrutiny by government regulators, they are being a little pickier and taking longer to review ads. Be patient, your ad should be up and running soon after submission.

After you've run the campaign, that is just the beginning. Once someone likes your Facebook page, every time you post on it they see it on their feed. So you're going to want to keep generating content on your blog and YouTube and routinely post it to your Facebook page, at least 2-3 times per week. This will keep your prospects interested and actively engaged, and prompt them to share your posts and get you some organic prospects free of charge.

Ad Rejections

Sometimes Facebook will reject an ad. In these situations, it's best to work with the reviewers rather than try arguing. The first step is to carefully review the reasons that they give for disapproving the campaign. To give a specific example, recently I was advertising a diet product and a training course for starting an online business. Both were rejected.

The reason given for the diet ad was that the ad asked a question about weight loss. While it's ridiculous, Facebook said that asking the question was an invasion of privacy. I could have tried arguing, but instead, I reworked the question into a statement that was more indirect. They approved the ad.

The second campaign ran into trouble because Facebook didn't really understand what the training was about. They said that ads promoting "get rich quick schemes" and MLM or work from home were not allowed. So before resubmitting the ad, which drove traffic to a website, I put in an explicit disclaimer on the website that it was not a "get rich quick" method. I had also mentioned that you would work from home running an internet business in the ad but removed that text. Then I wrote the Facebook review team and pointed them to this disclaimer, and then also explained that the training was not an MLM scheme and why. I also made it clear I had removed the work from home reference, to show I was paying attention to what they were telling me. About an hour later the ad campaign was approved.

So if your advertisement is rejected, take a few minutes to review Facebook's ad policies and then write a calm and concise letter to the review team explaining why your ad campaign is compliant with their policies. If you have to make some adjustments to the ad text or your video/image, do so and let them know that you've made changes to bring the ad into compliance.

Remember – it's their platform and they make the rules, and our ability to advertise on their platform is a privilege, not a right. So the review team is "always right", even if they are being ridiculous.

Summary

So now we've found out how to create a Facebook ad with an associated Facebook page. Remember that you are going to need a Facebook page, period, for all your advertising activities. Also remember that to get the most out of your campaigns, follow these steps:

- Create a blog. It doesn't have to be fancy, but just a place where you can park period content. But to launch post at least 7-10 articles. They don't have to be long, we're just creating them for the purpose of being able to put linked content on the Facebook page.
- Create a YouTube channel for your business, and upload 1-3 videos (tip-install VidIQ to your browser, it's free and gives you a lot of insight on YouTube including what keywords others are using).
- If you are not the creative type, Spend $50 to have freelancers on Fiverr write articles and make videos for you.
- At this point, create your Facebook page. Create ten individual posts for each article and video you created in the first two steps to give your page some content.
- Run your Facebook ad campaign for page likes.
- After you start building a following, keep posting material on the Facebook page, about 3 times per week.

CHAPTER 4
Targeting And A/B Testing

In the last chapter, we went through the steps required to set up your first ad. As part of that process, we touched on targeting. In this chapter, we're going to explore utilizing targeting in conjunction with testing. Although people usually say "A/B Testing" for our purposes it will really be A/Z testing and maybe beyond, depending on how many factors you want to vary.

The goal is to drive advertising costs down by increasing conversion rates. Facebook is really good for advertising, so you can just throw ads up and if they are reasonably targeted they are going to get page likes, web traffic, opt-ins or app installs, whatever the case may be in your particular set of goals. However, there is a huge difference in advertising budgets when you're talking about paying $1 to get someone to visit your web page versus paying $0.19.

For the purposes of targeting, we can break down several parts of the ad campaign that we need to look at.

Location

The first targeting strategy is the location. In one of my ad campaigns, I advertise a slot machine game that I made for the iPhone. These have international popularity, however, you make more money in some locations ("geos" in the lingo of global advertising) than in others. Another factor is that different cultures are going to respond to advertisements in different ways.

So it would be foolish to throw up a global campaign with the same ad creative, bid, and daily budget.

In my case, breaking down ads by location in the following way was the best approach. In other words – I would create ad campaigns for these locations, and then they would be varied in some way tailored to the local market:

- The United States and Canada
- Australia and New Zealand
- Hong Kong
- Japan
- United Kingdom
- Western Europe
- Mexico

So I'd need seven campaigns, not just one campaign, to advertise my game. Location may or may not impact your product or service. Let's suppose you're a real estate agent in Phoenix. You could advertise in Phoenix hoping to find clients to come to look at your house.

Or – you could advertise in Phoenix, in the entire state of Arizona, and also nationwide. The first step in designing an ad campaign might be to look up the top five states that provide immigration to Arizona. I'm not going to actually do it for the book, but you might find that the states were something like California, New York, Pennsylvania, Texas, and Ohio.

This suggests that we might want to run ads in those states as well. At first, it's going to be a little bit rough. But here are some things you could consider if you were setting up these campaigns.

First, you create a campaign and set the location targeting to the state of New York. Then under interests, you add the following:

- Arizona
- Moving company
- Real estate broker
- Real estate
- Coldwell Banker
- Century 21

Notice that by tying these interests together, we might be able to put together an audience made up of people living in New York who may be interested in buying a home in Arizona.

On your first run, it's going to be a little rough. Kind of like throwing darts in the ocean. However, over time you're going to start picking up interested customers. And the important thing about this –while those prospects are important too – is creating a database of characteristics of people responding to the ad. You can then use this to create a lookalike audience. We discuss that in detail in chapter 9, for now, we just need to note that this is something you can build up with the data.

Without actually running these ad campaigns it's hard to know if creating separate campaigns for all five states is really necessary, and that might make the demo too small. This is something that is going to vary considerably depending on your product or service and target demo. So in this case, we might instead create just three campaigns:

- Phoenix metro
- Arizona statewide
- Out of state targeting NY, CA, OH, etc.

I'd be inclined to limit my out of state targeting to the top five states, however. Advertising in Utah or Colorado if hardly anyone moves from those states to Arizona would be wasting effort and advertising funds.

Basic Demographics

The next thing to look at for targeted ads is age, gender, and language (if applicable). The reality is that different age groups and genders respond differently to advertising pitches. Also, younger people (under the age of 30) are more likely than other age groups to be on Instagram. If your product or service targets people under the age of 30, you might want to create a separate campaign for that age group, so that you can create one for older demographics that leaves Instagram out. If you are advertising beauty products, you probably don't want to waste time and money showing the ads to males.

It may be that you don't need to break out ad campaigns to specifically target these base demos. But if you feel a need to do so,

32

you will need to create campaigns broken down by each group PLUS the location breakdowns above, if you made them. So using our previous example, we could create ad sets in the following way:

- Phoenix Metro, males
- Phoenix Metro, females
- Arizona statewide, males
- Arizona statewide, females
- Out of state, males
- Out of state, females

If you were selling a home, then the 13-29 age group probably isn't relevant. So you'd probably want to set your age to be at least 30 in this case. If you were advertising apartment rentals, then you'd be more likely to advertise to 18-29-year-olds and block people 35 and older instead.

On the other hand, if you were marketing a video game, then including the younger demographic would be more important. Note that Facebook may have certain restrictions for advertising to those under the age of 18. That can come off as exploitative, so I'd advise in not doing it unless you have a product specifically targeted at that age group.

Placements

Depending on your main target demo, you might look at placements as well. We've mentioned several times that Instagram may not be suitable for many types of ad campaigns. Another thing to consider is placement on mobile devices. Now it's true that millions of people over the age of 65 are using iPhones and iPads, but it's also true that someone 65+ is less likely than a young person to be doing so. Suppose that your real estate business was specifically targeted at retirees. Do you want to be showing all your impressions on iPhones? Maybe not – so in that case, it might be better to select Desktop for your selection of devices.

Of course, you should always let the market speak to you. So we've created this theory that people aged 65+ are not going to be on mobile very much and are more likely to respond to an ad targeted only at the desktop. The only way to really know is to run two campaigns. One that targets all devices, and one that specifically targets the desktop. Then the data will tell us if we need to make this distinction. We might even find that our hypothesis is false and that we actually need to advertise to people 65+ on mobile devices.

Budget Settings

When it comes to budget settings, there is only one area that we will look at for A/B testing. This is "Lowest Cost" (according to Facebook) and Bid Cap. You'll want to set up one campaign for each. For the Lowest Cost, there isn't anything to do other than let it run. For bid cap, we might experiment with our choice of cap. Remember that you should probably just ignore the suggestion that Facebook gives you. My suggestion is put in the price that you want to pay. If you run the campaign and it doesn't get any results or show enough impressions, then slowly raise the bid. Start with your ideal price.

Using the example of app installs, I know from experience that 85 cents are a workable price in the United States. However, if I were setting up a brand new campaign, I'd start off low – say 55 cents – and see how it worked out. Assuming that it started off really slow, each day I would raise the bid 10 cents. By the end of the first week, the campaign should be in a situation where it's doing well at a price that is far more acceptable than that proposed by Facebook.

Here are the rules of thumb to follow:

- Never accept the suggested bid cap that Facebook gives you.
- Start low, and don't expect results immediately.
- Slowly raise the bid, about 10 cents per day (you can even try 5 cents per day)
- When the ad is delivering a level of results you want, then leave the bid cap alone and start raising your daily budget.

Creative Types

When discussing ad creatives, there are two ways that you can vary the ad for targeting. These are:

- Creative types
- The actual creatives themselves

The first choice for creative types is whether or not we are going to use a static image or a video. Using a static image certainly works – however, the trend is definitely toward video. It's not very hard to make a good video. You might make a video of yourself just using the webcam making a pitch for some offer. Or you could make a slideshow on Keynote or Powerpoint and record it with narration. If you are not up to making your own videos, hire someone on Fiverr to make a video for you at low cost.

But if the video is out of the question, you can go with an image.

The ideal situation is to do more A/B testing. Create an advertising campaign that uses an image, and then create one that has a video. Then run them for a week and compare results.

Now, of course, you can see that the deeper we get, the more reasons there are to do A/B testing. Are you going to stop at one video? Hopefully, you don't have that constraint – but if you do we hope you are able to launch your campaign anyway. However, in the ideal case, you're definitely going to want to be able to test multiple videos in your ad campaigns. You should have at least three different videos to test. But the more the better.

You are also going to want to test them against the other breakdowns you've used. It might be more productive to have different videos that target males, and females for example. Or maybe if you're targeting by age group you'll have different videos for major age breakdowns. At least 18-29 versus 35+.

Using our real estate example, you can see that you're probably going to be running a totally different advertisement that targets people already living in the Phoenix metropolitan area as opposed to out of state residents. And when targeting out of state residents, you might need a different ad that targets someone moving from New York as opposed to someone moving from California. For someone moving from New York, you might want to be emphasizing the weather, and how it rarely if ever snows in Arizona. But that really isn't much of a selling point for someone coming from California, so for them, you might emphasize the lower cost of living, less pollution, and maybe less traffic. The specifics here aren't important, what is important is that you start thinking about how to develop advertising creatives that address the special needs of your different targets.

Headlines and Text

By now, your head may be spinning. We've already built up a pretty large number of ways that ad campaigns can and should be varied. Now we have two more – testing headlines and text.

The first thing is to look at the text. You can add a significant amount of text, so don't feel you have to restrict it to just a couple of lines. You don't want to overwhelm the prospect with the ad, it's just a vehicle to get them on your pages or captured as a lead. But you can write as much text as you believe is necessary.

Remember that Facebook is *interactive*. For that reason, one thing I like to do is make the ads in such a way as to encourage interaction. The more you do that, you start getting comments and the increased engagement leads to more shares, helping get you free traffic and publicity.

A simple way to do that is to ask a question. For an ad I might create for my slot machine game, I might say:

How would it feel to win 10 million bonus coins?

The type of question you ask will depend on the target demographic. Yes, I know there are some stereotypes but there is some truth to them too. Women, on average, are going to respond more to questions that ask about emotions and feelings. It turns out that players of slot machine games are around 60-65% female, and so I tailor my ads with that in mind. But asking the question is likely to get some people viewing the ad to post a response.

Your prompt doesn't have to be a question. It can be a statement that helps someone visualize something.

For the Arizona ad, we could make an ad targeting people moving from New York making a statement such as:

Imagine enjoying snow free moderate winters.

If the person viewing the ad is thinking of moving from upstate New York to the southwest, this statement is going to immediately trigger an interest – and help them visualize themselves enjoying January in 65 degree sunny temperatures.

Another copywriting technique that people use is a phrase that implies some type of unknown secret is being revealed that will solve a problem someone is having. This should be followed by a statement of benefits and a time within which the people can meet their goal. It should also include the word "guaranteed".

For example:

Discover the new low carb diet guaranteed to make you lose 14 pounds in the first two weeks, sleep better, and have more energy than you've had in years.

Notice that we've implied that a secret is being revealed by using the word "Discover". Then we give three specific results – lose 14 pounds, sleep better, and have more energy. This information is provided with a specific time frame of two weeks.

There is less room for the headline, so I keep my questions or longer ad copy in the text section, and try to make my headlines impactful and short. The headline should take on a more mundane but important role of giving a clear description of what you're offering or the type of business. Examples of headlines:

- New Slot Machine Game on iOS
- Bankruptcy Attorney with 20 Years Experience
- Custom Designed Handbags for Women

Now we aren't done. You're not going to come up with one clever statement or question – you're going to try coming up with five. And then we are going to A/B test all of them.

Carrying out you're A/B testing

After you've figured out all the variations you can test, then it's time to run your campaigns. You should probably have about 20 variations that you have to build into 20 different ad campaigns. Although Facebook lets you create multiple ad sets within a campaign and so on, I find it easier to just create the first campaign and then duplicate it so that I can see everything from the main screen. But you can do what works for you.

After you create your campaign, you will see it listed on the Ads Manager. Hover your mouse over it and you will see a *Duplicate* option. Click on it and Facebook will make a Duplicate for you. Open it up and give the campaign of the clone a new meaningful name. For example, if our first campaign was called Real Estate – Phoenix Metro, we would create a duplicate and then name it Real Estate – New York.

After you've given it a name that identifies what you're varying, then edit the campaign to put your variation in. In this case, we'd go to Location and change it from Phoenix to the state of New York, and then we'd go to the Engagement/Creative Section to make changes that are appropriate for the testing.

The program you should follow goes like this:

1. Create your 20 clones and set all the variations you want to test.
2. Set your daily budgets low – you can try $3-5.
3. Let the campaigns run for at a minimum of 3 days. Five days is best.
4. At the end of five days, analyze your campaigns.

After five days, you'll want to weigh the following items:

- The number of results per campaign.
- Total money spent.
- Cost per result.
- Click through rate and other factors might also be important, but the top three are the most important.

For the real estate ads, we should have created a few ads that target New York residents looking to move. They might vary by text or video creative. Some will perform, some will not.

- Turn off all ads that don't perform.
- Any ad that has a cost per result of more than $1 after five days should be shut down.
- Any ad that isn't getting more than 5 results per day should be shut down.

If you started with 20 ads, you can probably whittle it down to 5-8 ads by the end of the week. So now you have ad campaigns that should be able to work for you. At the low budgets, we've set they probably aren't bringing in nearly as many prospects as you'd like. So the next step is to start ramping up budgets:

- Increase your budget slowly – about 15% per day.
- Leave it set for at least 24 hours before raising again.
- Keep raising it until you're getting the number of impressions and results that you're seeking.

This procedure works. If you're brand new, it might take a few rounds to make it work but if you follow it over time you'll be an expert at getting low-cost prospects for your business.

CHAPTER 5
Audience Insights

In this chapter, we are going to discuss an important research tool that you can use to create various "audiences" to target with your ad campaigns. Facebook calls its *Audience Insights*. To find it, click on *Ads Manager* in the upper left corner of the window. Then you should see the following options:

- Ads Manager
- Analytics
- Audience Insights

Click on Audience Insights and a new screen should open. The first thing you are going to see though is a little popup window that has two choices:

- Everyone on Facebook
- People connected to your page

After you've been running ads for a while, you may want to select *People Connected to your page*. However, that isn't going to be useful at the beginning. You will need to collect a significant amount of data before Facebook can show you that information. So for now, we'll start with Everyone on Facebook.

Location

The page is divided into three major sections. First, call your attention to the left sidebar. This is a toolset you can use to filter out your demographics. It's not all that different from the filtering options that we've seen when creating our first advertisement. At the very top of the left sidebar, you will see a *Locations* tab. The default selection is going to be your home country, for me, it says the United States. If you hover your mouse above the input box but below the default location you will see that you can switch to exclusion targeting – if that is useful. The default setting is inclusion, so when it shows the United States it shows all people living in the United States.

If you click on the Exclude option, this will open up a popup window. So for example, I could start with the United States, and then exclude California if I chose to do so.

Just to the right of Location, you will notice that it gives audience size and age and gender demographics. Just for fun, try deleting the United States or your home country and see how the data changes. When you have the United States selected, for example, you will see:

- Audience size 200-260 million active people
- 54% women, 46% men

If you delete the United States, you'll see the global data:

- Now it changes to more than 1 Billion active people
- The demographic has shifted, now it's 57% men, and 43% women

So you can see that demographics may vary considerably from country to country. If you are doing advertising internationally this could be a very important piece of information.

Age and Gender

Returning to the left sidebar, the next thing we find below location is Age and Gender. You can select a specific age range, gender, or some combination thereof. There are many ways in which you will find this helpful as we'll see, but on a gross level, it will give you a measure of your market size (for example how many women aged 35+ are on Facebook).

You can also target by moving your mouse over the graphics in the center of the page. Facebook has broken down age and gender demographics into the key marketing groups. This information will tell you what percentage of Facebook users are in each group. Something interesting to note for example – is that the percentage of women on Facebook in the United States breaks down with about the same number aged 18-24 and 65+ - at 14% and 13%, respectively.

Before we look at more items on the left sidebar, let's take a look at the center of the screen. Facebook has broken down the demographics in the following additional ways:

- Relationship status
- Education level
- Job title

So for example, we find that 53% of women in the United States who are active Facebook users are married, and 62% of them have attended college. If you zoom in on the 45-54 age group by clicking on the bar in the Age/Gender chart area, you find that 69% are married and 60% have attended college. In contrast, among those aged 25-34 only 42% are married but 67% have attended college. These bits of information may be useful for your business activities.

You can scroll down to the bottom and look at Job Title for some more interesting information. It will tell you what percentage of the selected demographic has what job title, and how that compares to the overall Facebook audience.

For example, for females aged 35-44 living in the United States, we find that 12% work in "community and social services" which compares to 7% working in this field for the Facebook audience at large. If you switch to men on Facebook aged 35-44 who live in the United States, you'll see that 4% work in the community and social services. This illustrates how you might analyze the characteristics of audiences to better target your advertising.

You can also select different cities to see how the demographics change. So using our previous example in the last chapter where we considered real estate advertising for Phoenix and reaching out of state, we might check the demographics of people in the different areas first, to get ideas about how we are going to target our advertising and what creatives we would consider using.

Interests

Now, return to the left sidebar and click on the Interest textbox. This actually works in a similar fashion to browsing interests when you create an ad campaign. When you first click on it, if you don't type anything in it will populate with a large number of categories that you can browse to see if they are of any relevance.

There are two ways you can explore interests to create audiences. You can do the browsing method and select among the given categories. These include:

- Business and Industry: You could use this to try and target people that worked in specific occupations. Examples – Banking or engineering.
- Entertainment: Includes a wide variety of entertainment categories. For example, you can select games and then pick out people that like to play board games, or people that like casino games. You can also select other options such as movies, TV, live events.
- Family and Relationships: Has multiple important categories. Including Motherhood, Dating, Family, Friendship, etc. Suppose you had a book on dating – you could use this to target your demographic.
- Fitness and Wellness: In this section, you'll find different physical activities listed, like weight training or yoga.
- Hobbies and Activities: Covers a wide range, from an interest in various kinds of pets to political activities.
- Shopping and Fashion: Includes Beauty, Clothing, Fashion Accessories, Shopping, and Toys.
- Sports and Outdoors: Includes outdoor recreation with subcategories and various sports activities.
- Technology: Last but not least people obsessed with their electronic gadgets, or maybe people that work on them.

Note that many of the listings include lots of subcategories. From this listing, you can see that you can drill down quite a bit into many different characteristics that will help you target your advertising. For example, you could write a book on the PE or Professional Engineering exam, and then advertise it to engineers aged 25-44 in the United States (younger engineers will be less likely to already be PE's).

As we demonstrated when creating our first ad campaign, you aren't limited to these categories. You can drill down even more by simply typing in words or phrases that might be relevant. For example, if we were targeting people interested in "Dating", we could use the browsing capability to select that. However, if you type "Dating" in the input box you see a lot more options pop up:

- Online dating service
- Speed dating
- Interracial dating
- Etc.

What approach should you use? Both of course! So select Dating from browse, and then type in dating and select the relevant interests. If we had an eBook we wanted to market to people interested in online, interracial dating, you can see that we could readily target them.

People Connected to Your Page

Just below the Interest section on the left side, we see an option to select either people connected to one of our Facebook pages or People Not Connected to one of our Facebook Pages. If you are just starting you're not going to have enough data for this, but once you build up a few thousand prospects you'll be able to utilize it. Well, of course, you can use people NOT connected to your Facebook page now because you probably don't have many that ARE connected.

So why utilize this? You don't want Facebook to be showing your ads to people who've already seen them and then opted in by liking your page already. So even if you only have a few users, you might want to select your page for People Not Connected to your Facebook page.

Advanced

Now let's take a look at the Advanced section, which is just below the Page option. This section covers the following areas:

- Language
- Relationship status
- Education
- Work
- Market Segments
- Parents
- Politics (US)
- Life Events

Each of these has multiple subcategories. For example, you can use it to drill down to people who report being single, employed in healthcare and medical services, who are bilingual Hispanic females.

WOW!

Hope that makes your head spin. Remember where we began – talking about throwing up a TV ad that would show your video to everyone living in your hometown – and it would cost you a fortune.

Now for a few dollars, you can drill down big time.

Page Likes

Now return to the top of the page, and look at the tabs that run across the top of the middle section. Click on *Page Likes*.

This section is going to give you some ideas about what your targeted demographic is doing on Facebook in regard to what kinds of pages they are visiting and giving likes to. This information can be utilized to help tailor your messaging.

At the top, you'll see a listing of top categories. For my example, I selected women 25+ who play card games and work as engineers. When I look at categories, some of the items I see are Dollar

General, Betty Crocker, Pillsbury, and IKEA. All the items listed in this section are linked, so you can click on them to examine the page in question.

Below this list, you'll see a ranked list of page likes. In my case, the top-ranked page is Screaming Owl. I have no idea what that is so had to open the link to see it's a boutique shop. Other items listed include Big Lots, Toys "R" Us, and Dollar General.

You can change up your demographic to see how the page likes change. Simply switching to men – the boutique shop gets replaced by AR Armor, which is a shop that sells body armor! The second page listed is Alien Gear Holsters – which sells gun holsters.

On the far right, you will see column labeled *Affinity*. This will tell you how much more a given page is liked by your target demographic as compared to the general Facebook audience. For example, the 500 Armor page has an affinity of 55x. That means that the target demo I've selected is 55 times more likely to like the page than the general Facebook audience. It will also give you the total number of likes.

Reverse Engineering

Hopefully, so far we've illustrated how you can use Audience Insights to help you target your audience. But it also should get the wheels turning in your mind. You can reverse engineer and then *develop new products* to target different audiences – by looking at what they are already interested in. The power of the tools Facebook provides advertisers are frankly overwhelming. Knowing that men who are engineers (and a few other characteristics I selected).

Location

Now let's return to the tabs at the top of the page. If you click on the Location tab, you're going to see a listing of the top locations for your targeted demographic. This can be viewed as top cities, top countries, and top languages. For each location, you can hover your mouse over the bar and it will tell you the percentage of your

Facebook audience that is in that location, and how that compares to the overall Facebook audience. For my current selections, I find that my top location is Los Angeles. Surprisingly the numbers match up exactly – the proportion of users in Los Angeles in my target demo is the same as the proportion of overall Facebook users in Los Angeles. On the other hand, 1% of the target demo lives in Manhattan, as compared to 2% of all Facebook users.

Activity

Now let's click on the final tab, which is Activity. This tells us what sorts of things related to marketing and promotion the audience is engaged in – such as page likes, Ads clicked or comments posted. Below this, you will find device usage. We can actually use this to check the hypothesis I raised earlier. Remember I suggested that maybe people aged 65+ are more likely, perhaps far more likely to be using desktop computers. To find out for sure, I can filter the Facebook audience for ages 65+ here on Audience insights and then check the Activity tab. I find that:

- 54% are mobile only
- 33% are using mobile + desktop
- 12% are desktop only

Frankly, I find this a bit shocking – so the older people have gone a long way toward adopting mobile – and only a small minority are using Facebook on desktop only. So my assumption was totally wrong.

The lesson here is this – use Audience Insights to check any assumptions you make before creating your ads. Just for fun, let's bring up the 35-44 demographic. Here we find that:

- 69% are mobile only
- 29% are using mobile + desktop
- 3% are desktop only

So while the younger crowd is more oriented toward using mobile for Facebook than the 65+ group, the difference really isn't relevant since the proportion of those ages 65+ using only desktop computers for Facebook are a small minority.

Saving the Audience

Now that you've done all this hard work to put research into developing a useful audience and finding out what they're into, you're going to want to save it rather than just tossing it aside. To do this, go to the very top of the page where you'll see the following options:

- Create New
- Open
- Save
- More (includes Save As... and Take Tour)

Once you save an audience, then you can use it when you create new ad campaigns.

Creating an Advertisement

Now, you can return to the ads manager and create new ad campaigns that use your audience once you save it. However, you should notice that the green Create Ad button is found on the Audience Insights page. So you can go through the research steps and create your audience, save it, and then click on Create Ad and build your new ad campaign right there. So nice of Facebook to make it convenient to spend more money on their platform!

CHAPTER 6
Facebook Pixel

Now we approach the mysterious topic of the Facebook Pixel! We'll find out what the Facebook Pixel is when you want to use, why you want to use it, and if you're going to use it at all.

In short, the Facebook Pixel is an analytics tool you can use to track the behavior of your prospects and customers on your website. It can be used to track their behavior and to determine whether or not you're targeting the right people with your ads. You will also be able to determine if Facebook is really helping your website traffic when you've got traffic coming to the site from multiple sources. The "Pixel" is just a small bit of code that will connect your website to your Facebook ads account. The Facebook Pixel, once installed, can then be "triggered" when people using your website take various actions, like signing up on a form or buying a product.

The pixel will collect a wide range of data, including page headers, IP addresses, and button clicks.

Furthermore, you can create ads that target different actions taken by users on your website. For example, some people might visit your website without actually making a purchase. The Facebook pixel can be used to target those near converting customers who are interested but didn't buy. Maybe they didn't buy because the price is too high for them, so you could run an ad campaign targeting that group offering a coupon code for a reduced price.

You can even target people that engage in actions like watching a video – and maybe they don't finish watching the entire video. Gathering the user data from the pixel you can create an ad campaign reminding them to finish the video.

Another application of the Facebook Pixel is using it to target people who've purchased. Maybe you want to offer them an upsell option. Using the pixel data you can run a campaign offering the upsell.

Facebook provides a complete listing of "standard events" that can be used with the pixel. These include Add to Cart, Add payment information, Contact, Lead/Form Submission, and several others. You can view the entire listing here:

https://business.facebook.com/business/help/402791146561655

If you're using Facebook to drive mobile app installs, then you're not going to be thinking about the Facebook pixel at all. To run ads for app installs, you'll need to have integrated the Facebook SDK in your app, and that will essentially play the role of the Facebook pixel for you in that context.

OK so now let's turn our attention to the cases when you might not need to use it. For ads generating page likes – you don't need to worry about it because you're working inside Facebook. For all other ads, however, the Facebook pixel might be important.

First a caveat – you are not required to use a Facebook Pixel. However, if you don't use it, then you're going to miss out on a lot of information that it can collect. It just depends on your situation.

Let's take a couple of examples where you might be driving traffic outside Facebook but you don't really need to use the Facebook pixel. The first case we'll consider is email marketing. If you aren't familiar with email marketing, what this involves is driving traffic to a "landing page" which you use to entice people to give you their email address. Typically you'll offer them some kind of freebie in exchange for the email address. If you are marketing says a course on ketogenic dieting, then you can offer them a short ten-page cookbook with ketogenic compliant recipes in exchange for the email address. To do this, you add a landing page to your website or use some kind of page builder that can be linked up to an email list provider like Aweber. The landing page will have a small amount of copy together with a form for people to fill out to get their gift. Once they give you their email address, then you can start sending them emails to sell them on your product.

To do this type of promotion, you will create a Facebook ad campaign and select Traffic, and you'll give the landing page URL as the destination page for the campaign. So when a user clicks after viewing your ad then it will take them right to the landing page where they can sign up to join your email list or simply ignore you.

OK so why wouldn't you want to use the Facebook Pixel in this case? The answer is you don't really need it. All the information you need for this type of campaign is going to be contained both at Facebook and at your email list provider. The two pieces of information of interest for us here would be the number of clicks from our ad campaign, and the number of people who sign up once they hit the landing page. So for the time period that you're running your campaign, you will collect a given number of email addresses that are reported in Aweber or Mail Chimp say, and then you can compare that to the number of clicks your Facebook ad generates. Then you can determine the number of people who visited the page and the number who converted into leads.

So far what we're saying is you don't need a Facebook pixel to gauge the success or failure of your ad campaign. However, there may be cases when running a lead generation campaign like this that you will want to use the Facebook pixel.

The scenario which was described above works fine provided that Facebook is the only ad campaign that you're running. Suppose that instead you're running a lead generation campaign but advertising simultaneously on Facebook, Bing, and YouTube. Then you might have a problem. Maybe you're getting a good amount of organic traffic. In either case, when people start signing up for your email list, you won't know where they came from – so you won't have an idea as to whether or not the Facebook ad campaign was a complete waste of time.

So if you're a beginner and you don't want to dive into the Facebook Pixel right away – and that's fairly understandable since it seems complex – provided that you are not running a bunch of simultaneous campaigns on other networks, you may be able to get away with it, at least for a while.

However, if you want to find out what activity on your website is being driven by Facebook, then installing the Facebook pixel is a very good idea.

Another example where the Facebook Pixel will be useful is for an e-commerce site. The Facebook Pixel can not only help you determine where people visiting your site are coming from and hence whether or not the Facebook ad campaigns are working out for you, but you can detail the activity of people once they get on your site. For example, you can determine whether someone:

- Jumped on your site without adding any products to the shopping cart.
- If they added a product to the shopping cart, then left your site without closing the sale.
- If they entered the payment method and other info, and either bought or didn't buy.
- Product searches.
- Actual purchases.

This can help you determine whether or not advertising on Facebook is something that's worth doing for you. However, I take the position that advertising on Facebook is always worth doing. If it's not working out for you, what you need to do is revisit your ad targeting and make adjustments.

Creating the Pixel

You can open the Ads manager to create your Facebook Pixel. This is accessed from the Ads Manager drop-down list in the upper left corner. Click it open and select "All Tools". You will find "Pixels" under the events manager in the third column on the right-hand side.

Facebook has recently updated the page, so at the time of writing it says "welcome to the new Pixels Page". In the middle of the page, there is a green button that says "Create Pixel". Click on it.

A dialog will open that will give you three options.

- Connect to a Partner Platform (formerly the vague 'tag manager')
- Manually Install the Code Yourself.

- Email instructions to a developer.

The third option is pretty self-explanatory. If you have a developer that manages your website, then you can have Facebook email them the code with instructions and they can install it on your website for you.

Connect to a Partner Platform

A partner platform is some kind of website you're using that has worked with Facebook to help integrate Pixels. For example, several e-commerce platforms have integrated with Facebook to allow you to do this. Some of these include Shopify, WooCommerce, 3dCart, and Ticketmaster. Several site development tools can be integrated with the Facebook pixel used as a partner platform. These include Wordpress, Weebly, Wix, Drupal, and Squarespace.

If you are utilizing Leadpages for email lead generation, then you can use the Connect to a Partner Platform method to integrate your signup forms.

The specific instructions on how to integrate the Facebook pixel will vary by partner. If you are using one of the partners, you can look it up on the Facebook help page listed here:

https://business.facebook.com/business/help/117921076546889 4

Click on the link for your partner and it will give you instructions. If yours is not listed then you can access the help for your given platform.

Let's take a look at a couple of examples to see what's involved. First, we'll check WordPress since so many people use the platform for their websites. For WordPress, the Facebook Pixel is built as a WordPress plugin. So you simply download the zip file, and then open up your WordPress Dashboard and go to install and activate the plugin just like you would any other plugin. Now that was pretty simple, right?

For many of the other partners, you will open the Events Manager which is found from the Facebook Ads Manager drop-down menu (this is how you will do most of them). When you open it up, you will see a menu on the left-hand side. Click on Partner Integrations. Then a series of buttons will be displayed in the middle of your screen where you can select the appropriate partner for your situation.

For example, if you have a Shopify account, then you can connect it inside the Facebook Events Manager by clicking the blue Connect Account button.

On your own website

Integrating the Facebook Pixel on your own website isn't really that difficult, but of course, you should seek out developer assistance if you shy away from techie activities. If you are OK with doing it yourself, you can follow the instructions on this page:

https://business.facebook.com/business/help/952192354843755

CHAPTER 7
Introduction To Facebook Ads Manager

In this chapter, we will dive into the Facebook ads manager, which is the "dashboard" for your ad campaigns. The Facebook ads manager can be accessed on this web page:

https://business.facebook.com/adsmanager/

When you open the page, you'll see your ad campaigns listed in a series of rows on the left-hand side. You can click on an ad campaign on the list to View Charts, Edit, or Duplicate. To the right, you will see three tabs: Campaign, Ad Sets, Ads. Facebook has a three-level system.

- The campaign is a top-level
- A campaign can include one or more ad sets
- Each ad set can contain one or more ads

I like keeping things simple so always work at the campaign level. However, if you'd like to add multiple ad variations to one ad set and/or multiple ad sets to each of your campaigns, you can organize things that way. To view the ad sets for a single campaign, select it in the campaigns tab, and this will open the ad sets tab. Here you can duplicate an ad set. If you click on an ad set in the adsets listing, it will move to the ads tab and show you a listing of ads for that ad set. Here you can create new ads within the ad set. Charts can be viewed for campaigns and ad sets. You can also duplicate ads, edit, or view charts for them if you select the ads tab without selecting the ad sets tab.

To understand the different levels, we can start by opening up one campaign. When you do this the editor will slide open from the right-hand side. At the top level, you see the ad campaign. The campaign consists of the following information:

- Campaign Name
- Objective (i.e. page likes, app installs)
- Campaign spending limit (optional)

- Campaign budget optimization (optional)

At the ad set level, you see most of the details that you use to set up your ads. This includes:

- Associated Facebook page
- Budget and Schedule
- Audience (Location, Demographics, Interests)
- Optimization and Delivery

Now let's look at the lowest level, the ad level. This includes:

- Identity (Facebook page used with the ad)
- Creative
- Text and headline
- Call to action (if applicable)

You can duplicate ads within an adset and then use different creatives or test different headlines and text to gauge performance.

Charts

Charts can be viewed to determine performance at the campaign level, ad set level, and ad level.

The charts are divided as follows. At the top, there are three tabs: Performance, Demographics, and Placement. Performance shows a graph with the time of results and cost per result. Demographics produces a bar chart showing age and gender breakdowns, with results and cost per result for every demographic slice. Finally, on the far right, we can look at placements. This shows reach, results, and amount spent for each of the major placements (Facebook, Instagram, Messenger).

Data in the Ads Manager

In addition to the charts, you can review tables of data in the ad manager. There is a long list of columns moving across the page left to right. You can see how many impressions your ad has, what the click-through rate is, the reach (number of people the ad was shown to), the results (page like, app install, etc.). If you look toward the right-hand side, there are two options labeled Columns and Breakdown. You can use Columns to specify what columns you want to be displayed on the screen. Breakdown lets you look at a large variety of data. For example, you can break it down by time frame, day, week, month, etc. You can look at delivery information, which will show you the data by age groups, time of day, gender, device, and so forth. Action will show you conversion device, and other information.

Reports

The last button on the right is Reports. You can have Facebook generate up to 25 different reports for your data. When you generate a report, it will open on screen where you can view the data. You can download it (for example as an Excel Spreadsheet or CSV file) or save it on Facebook.

Opportunities

Recently, Facebook also added another tab called "Opportunities' where you can find tips and other information.

CHAPTER 8
Analyzing Results

The key to having success with Facebook ads lies with analyzing the results, making adjustments, and killing ads when they are not working. Secondly, you will want to ramp up the campaigns that are working. We have already discussed the general procedure but let's outline it again here.

Begin by identifying variations that you want to look at targeting. You can start with a general advertisement and go from there. In fact, you should include a general advertisement in your campaign in case the variations you imagine that might be required really aren't valuable. Using the example of a slot machine game, at the beginning of the book we mentioned that slot machines are popular in multiple countries such as the United States, Canada, Australia, Hong Kong, Japan, and the United Kingdom. At first glance, you might think that different ads need to be set up for say Japan and the United States. And sometimes this is true, but it's not always true. Sometimes you can hit on an ad creative that just works. The only way to find out is to test, test, and test.

Continuing with the slot example, we can make a single ad with our favorite video creative and then simply show it across the board. Then we can set up ad campaigns for each individual country and then run those alongside it. At the week's end, we compare results. If there is no distinct advantage to specialized ads, we can kill them. If they perform worse, we definitely kill them.

The specialized ads might work in some cases but not in others. So maybe the same ad works in Japan and the United States, but it doesn't work in Hong Kong. In that case, then you'll want to work on tailoring an ad specifically for Hong Kong.

There may be other reasons to keep your campaigns separate, but for the most part, Facebook will let you break out reports that will let you break down things by location or gender. However, one reason that you may want to keep locations separate even though they may perform the same with the same interest targeting and ad creatives is that costs are different in different countries. This also means that rewards are different in different countries. You can take this same lesson to the bank for different states and cities in the United States too.

Let's have a look at it. The cost per acquisition may be about the same if you're running the same exact ad across multiple locations. But the rewards might be different. For example, in mobile games, you earn money through ads that you show inside your game and through in-app coin purchases. Some locations might tend toward more coin purchases than others. Japan is better than Hong Kong, and the United States is where the money is (relatively speaking). However, advertisers pay different rates based on the country. They may pay a lot more in the United States than they do in say Hong Kong or France. That means that the cost of acquisition needs to be lower in those countries.

Two things you need to look at to see if your campaigns are working are:

- Cost of acquisition of a new customer
- The average lifetime value of a user

So if I have a mobile game and the cost of acquisition of a customer is $0.90 and that customer will generate $2.50 in revenue, then that is a winning proposition. However, bundling locations in ad campaigns can cause problems. For example, in the United States, an average user might cost $0.95 to acquire, but they might on average bring in $4 in earnings. In Hong Kong, they might cost $0.85, but only bring in $1.25 in revenue.

The same thing might be in play for our real estate ad. You might easily acquire prospects from New York who are interested in moving to Arizona, maybe as easily as you're getting from people in California. But California is a lot closer, so in reality, it's a lot easier to make the move. So over time, you might find that you're making a lot more revenue from California residents but only occasional sales from New York residents. The sales from New York still add to your bottom line, so you don't necessarily want to cut them out. But maybe an approach you will take is keeping the campaigns separate and running a campaign aimed at NY residents that has a much smaller daily budget.

Testing Your Campaigns

So to review, you'll need to figure out what variations you're going to run on your campaigns. It can be varying demos, interests, or just changing up creatives. The goal is to throw everything out there and then find out what works and what doesn't.

You can find out what works by running the campaigns for a week with very small budgets. In my opinion, below $3 per day is too small, but $10 a day is too large. The more you spend the more information you're going to get, but about $5 a day for a week should get you enough information to determine if a particular video or ad copy is working for you.

Data to Check on Ads Manager

You can determine whether an ad is working for you just by looking at a few parameters. The main ones to check are:

- Amount spent
- Impressions
- Clicks (or installs or page likes)
- Cost per result

You will want to know the click-through rate as well. This is simply clicks/impressions * 100. You can compare click-through rates between various ad campaigns and determine which ones are working and which ones are not working as far as generating the response to go to your site or page, to take that initial step of taking action.

Of course cost per result is an important parameter. If you are in a new business, and you really don't know the lifetime value of a customer, then you're not really going to be sure if a given cost per result is acceptable or not, however, what you can do is compare across ad campaigns to see what's working.

Now if you go to the Columns button and select Delivery, you can get the cost per 1,000 impressions of the ad. It's important to compare this cost across campaigns as well. However, note that one impression doesn't mean one person. The number of people is given by Reach. Some people might get more than one impression for whatever reason.

Another parameter to look at is Columns □Engagement. This will let you see the cost per click. Targeting and Creative will bring many of these measures together in a single display, showing you the cost per result, cost per 1,000 impressions, click through rate, and cost per click.

Even if you set up all your ads with the same exact budget – and that is what you should do – you might find some ads get a lot more impressions than others. This might happen because of demographic choices or interests that you've selected. If an ad is really sluggish with impressions, that is telling you that you will need to open it up a bit – possibly widening the demographics, location, or adding more interests (or reducing the interests).

Killing Your Ads

After the five-day period is up, it's time to kill all the ads that are not working. Simply shut them off. This can be done by toggling the button on the far left of the listing. Keep in mind that you can turn things off at every level. So if you have multiple ad sets and ads, be mindful of what you are really shutting off.

Next Steps

The next step is the ramp-up phase. This can work in two ways, the first is mandatory. To ramp up, begin increasing your daily budget. Never increase by more than 15% per day. So we will go like this – assuming that the trial period was set to $5 Daily Budget.

- Day 1: $5,75
- Day 2: $6.61
- Day 3: $7.60
- Day 4: $8.74

- Day 5: $10.05

How high you go after this depends on how many ads your running and what kind of daily budget you can absorb. However, if you're after a large number of prospects a $10 budget probably won't cut it, and you'll need to keep increasing until you get to $40 and above.

A word of warning about budget increases. For some reason, the Facebook system seems to respond better to gradual budget increases. So you aren't going to want to move from $5 to $40 or $100 in one shot. You will probably find it doesn't work. Take it gradually – soon enough you'll be at your spending goal.

Issues with bid caps

Bid caps can work in a funny way. You might find – but this depends on a huge number of factors so maybe you won't – that setting a bid cap you hardly get any traffic. In one test I did, using app installs where bid cap is replaced by an equivalent cost per install – I set a low price of 75 cents. Not much happened. I kept raising the daily budget.

It finally worked – but I had to set the daily budget at $400.

That might sound scary – it isn't. At $400 the campaign was still proceeding at its glacial pace. It opened it up enough so it brought in 20-30 installs per day, and I was happy to have them at that low cost   per   install.

This may happen to you or it may not, since there are so many factors that will influence how many impressions a given ad campaign is going to get. However, you can test the high budget if you are running into something like that which just isn't doing anything. Just keep a very close eye on it so that you can shut off the campaign if it starts spending in an out of control fashion.

Cloning

Years ago cloning showed much promise when Dolly the sheep was born. We haven't been overrun with clones, but the good news is you can clone your Facebook ad campaigns. They don't call it cloning, they call it duplicate. It's a tool that can come in handy to ramp things up.

Suppose you have a campaign with a daily budget of $20 and you want to spend $100 a day, and that campaign is working really well. Instead of gradually raising the budget, you can make five copies of it and run them simultaneously. That will help you get from there to here a lot faster. It's a technique that has worked for me many times.

CHAPTER 9
Traffic Vs. Page Likes

If you're new to Facebook advertising then you might find the types of ad campaigns a little fuzzy. We can generate traffic in a lot of different ways, you can use a lead generation campaign for example. Or you can simply use a traffic campaign that sends people to your lead generation site. Those kinds of distinctions aren't really important but the other two differ from page likes. Why would you want to use one and not the other?

Page Likes Advantages and Disadvantages

We've been through some of the advantages, but let's review them here. When you run a campaign for page likes, it's not a one-time thing. It's a connection that you're making to the client. This brings up an important point:

Use your Facebook page.

As the marketer, you don't want to just set up a Facebook page and leave it sitting there. Every time that you post on the Facebook page – it's going to show up on the feeds of people that liked your page.

In a sense, a page like is sort of like an email list. Way back when, in the early days of the internet, web marketing worked like this:

- Set up a one-page sales letter with an order button.
- Run a Google AdWords campaign that sent it traffic.

Unfortunately, two things happened. The first was Google got on its high horse and decided that it didn't like those kinds of sales pages. It wanted content, and it saw those pages as basically content free. To Google, they were evil sales pitches taking advantage of people.

Also, people began to get more skeptical. So a single sales page wasn't working as well as it had in the past.

These two developments were the birth of email marketing. The new strategy was this:

- Create a content-based website, so that Google would not "slap" you. It might include 20 pages of articles.
- Create an opt-in form on your website. People would sign up for an email newsletter in exchange for a free gift of some kind.
- Then you send the prospects a series of automated emails, giving them occasional offers to buy.

After this, things evolved again with the "landing page", which is a web page devoted to nothing more than collecting someone's email address in exchange for some kind of free gift.

Now fast forward to Facebook taking over the world. With a Facebook page, you essentially have a similar kind of setup. The Facebook page is acting as an email list, in giving you a way to communicate directly to your prospects and doing it on a regular basis.

Of course, there is no auto-responder. So you're going to have to keep your Facebook page live by routinely posting on it. When doing so you might want to occasionally slip in opportunities to buy products. If you're selling digital products, you can include a link to your sales page in a Facebook posting. You can occasionally hard sell it, but be careful with this, you don't want people to unlike your page – so only do that sparingly.

So in short, Facebook page likes to build up a customer or prospect database that you're in regular communication with. So what are the downsides?

The problem with this setup is that it's all too easy to like a posting on Facebook. So some person is scrolling through their feed, and they see your ad. Maybe it has a video they check out and they think it's cool – so they click on the like button.

But it really didn't mean all that much to them.

A large fraction of your page likes is going to be from people who aren't all that serious about spending money on your product or service. So you're going to have to get a lot of likes in order to start generating money from it. Until then, it might amount to a mere popularity contest.

Let's not get too down with this talk – having a Facebook page and getting page likes is still very useful. But don't rely on it.

Which brings us to traffic. You have a website up for whatever reason. Maybe you're selling t-shirts. Maybe you're an attorney with an informational site. Either way, your ultimate goal is getting customers on your website, not interacting with them on Facebook.

One way you can do this of course – is to post links to your site on the Facebook page. Earlier we recommended having a blog. You can integrate it with your main site, and many providers like Shopify already have a blog built-in. So you can post articles on your main site and then post them to the Facebook page.

Traffic Campaigns

However, this should work in concert with a traffic campaign. There are a couple of ways to drive traffic. Using the attorney example, you could explicitly advertise for bankruptcy services in your Facebook ad, and make it clear that clicking on the link would take a person to a page where they could contact you or sign-up on a form to be contacted.

If you are selling a digital product, then you can use Facebook advertising in roughly the same way you'd use Google AdWords. That is, the goal would be to take them to a landing page where they sign up for your email newsletter. I know, that is kind of a drag, you might have been hoping the Facebook page would help you get away from all that tedious stuff. The bottom line though is that email marketing is still the go-to technique for generating leads.

You can also do cold traffic, say to your t-shirt sight. That should be simple enough, you can have a good ad which shows the t-shirt with a sales offer. Better yet, use a carousel ad that mixes up videos of models wearing your t-shirts together with still shots of the shirt. When they click on the ad, they go right to your Shopify listing for the shirt.

Cold traffic is as risky as it ever was. However, Facebook works a lot better than using say Bing or Google Adwords, because you can show them the product in a 2-minute video before they click the link to visit your website.

Traffic vs. Page Likes

So when it comes down to it, which method is better? Chances are you're going to want to do both. While a lot of prospects that you're going to acquire from page likes are not going to be all that serious – liking a page doesn't take as much effort as signing up for emails, and your email prospects have to confirm their subscription, that second step weeds out a lot of people – the reality is a lot of people signing up for email newsletters aren't all that serious either. Think about how many promotional emails you probably get in your own inbox. How many of those do you bother opening? Probably a small fraction of them.

The best approach to marketing is to use as many avenues that you can. Page likes can be had for dirt cheap prices. So you may as well build up an audience with them. And since the old methods still work, you should also utilize traffic campaigns.

CHAPTER 10
Lookalike Audiences

So far we've seen many powerful features that are available to Facebook advertisers. You can target by age, by location, by gender, by occupation, by interest, and so forth. Now we come to the most powerful of all – the lookalike audience. The lookalike audience is the nuclear bomb of advertising.

Lookalike audiences can be developed in one of two ways. Or maybe we should say they can be had in one of two ways. You can buy or obtain the data you need for a lookalike audience from a broker or from someone who markets a related product or service – in the event, they are willing to sell or share it. In this case, you will upload the data to your Facebook account. Facebook is going to ask you about it, and what you should do is be honest and tell them that it's from a partner.

The data itself is not the lookalike audience. What the data will do is help Facebook create an entirely new list of customers that are Basically the same as the people in the data you provide. Although we view ourselves as thoughtful, independent, and smart actors, the scary thing is if we share a lot of characteristics we're going to buy the same stuff. Robotically. If you're doing marketing – take advantage of it!

Facebook probably has secret formulas, and we don't know what their secret sauce is. However, there are a few things we can look at that Facebook uses to create the lookalike audience:

- Age distribution
- Percent of males and females
- Device usage
- Income distribution
- Locations
- Occupations
- Page likes
- Interests

So if we're selling Chevy trucks and just starting out, we might contact the dealer on the other side of town and ask him for a database of his customers. In the old days he might have told us to get lost, but today you can assure him that you're not actually going to contact a single customer on his list. You just want to find out how old they are, and what pages they liked on Facebook.

We don't know how that would really work out, but let's say that the dealer agrees to sell you a list of 5,000 people for $250. All he is going to provide you is their name and email address.

It doesn't sound like much – but that's all Facebook needs to get to work.
When you upload the data, Facebook is going to use its system and all the data it has collected over the years to compile a list of customers – that didn't buy from your dealer on the other edge of town – but who are similar in every respect. That is your lookalike audience.

When you advertise to a lookalike audience, that is as if you have optimized your ad campaigns by running them for the past 6 months. You'll find that the performance of ads that use a lookalike audience outstrip those that don't by a massive margin. These will be your highest value customers.

You don't have to buy or borrow a database of people to create a lookalike audience. You can also create them from the data that you're generating in your own ad campaigns. You can use people who've liked your Facebook page to create a Lookalike audience. Although that will be your data alone, it takes time. From my experience, I'd recommend 5,000 people to create a good lookalike audience. You need to reach a certain threshold in order to be able to get enough data on demographics etc. in order to create a new list of similar people that will be responsive.

Another way you can create your own lookalike audience is to generate an email list using traffic campaigns. If you've had an online presence, you might already have one. So if you've been advertising your Chevy trucks online outside Facebook for years until now, and you've collected thousands of names and email addresses on your signup form, then you already have a base list of people with characteristics that are going to be associated with people who are interested in buying Chevy trucks. You can upload that list to Facebook and have it go to work to create an audience that you can then hit with Facebook ads. Some services, like Mail Chimp, have been set up so that you can simply import directly from Mail Chimp to Facebook.

Conversion rates using lookalike audiences can be astoundingly good, which means that the cost per result will be remarkably cheap. On a recent campaign using lookalike audiences I was able to get my cost of acquisition of new customers down to less than 20 cents.

That seems like it's almost back to the old days on Google in 2003 when you could advertise for pennies on the dollar.

Approaching Others for Data

Believe it or not, you may be able to get other people to share their data. You can put together a nice email explaining what you're interested in and ask if they are willing to share it. You can also try asking them if they will sell it. Most people are going to ignore you, that is a fact of life in a situation like this. But you're probably going to get lucky a few times and dig up people that are willing to give you some data or sell it to you. In your email, you might explain that a Facebook lookalike audience will not actually use their customers, and you can sign an agreement specifying that you won't contact their customers via the provided email (unless the customer happens to come to you some other way, of course). Since Facebook is taking the data and generating a new set of people from it (and the generated audience is a much larger size), you're not really using the customers themselves.

If you're willing to spend money, then you can search on the web for data brokers that can supply you with names and email addresses of people that have bought certain products. Just be careful if taking this approach as you're going to want to make sure you get recent and updated lists and not emails from ten years ago.

Uploading Your Data

Go to the Facebook Ads Manager drop-down menu. Select All Tools, and then click on Audiences. This will bring up a new screen showing any saved audiences you already have. In the upper left, there is a blue button labeled "Create Audience". Click on this button. You will see three options. These are Custom Audience, Lookalike Audience, and Saved Audience. Select Lookalike audience.

This will open a new window. You will specify the audience source, Audience location, and Audience size. To use data you have for upload, you click on Create New Source. There are two options:

- Custom Audience
- Custom Audience with LTV

We will explore the first option in the next section. In this section, we will select the Custom Audience with LTV.

This will open a new screen which will say Create a Data File Custom Audience with LTV. The top of the screen will show you information about creating a file that you can use to create a lookalike audience. It will say "Prepare a File with your Customer Data". It will also show the fields that are acceptable. The minimum that you need are:

- First Name
- Last Name
- Email address

This data is used to match up the people with their Facebook accounts. The data can be in an Excel spreadsheet but the first column on the left-hand side of your file must contain an integer that identifies the customer by row number. In other words, your file should have some structure like this:

1   Jane Doe jane.doe@gmail.com
2   Patrick Jones p.jones@swag.com
3   Betty Boop betty@boop.com

Column 1 is the number, column 2 is the first name, column 3 is the last name, and column 4 is an email address. A broker will know how to set this up properly for you. Upload your file and name the audience. You will have to specify some more information including location and audience size. Audience size is given as a percentage, I opt for 10%.

Other Sources

When you start off creating a custom audience, you will see two options, we explored custom audience with LTV in the last section. Now we will look at the plain custom audience. What this does is create a lookalike audience based on people that have visited your Facebook page or interacted with you some way on Facebook. Facebook sources that can be used are:

- Video
- Lead form
- Instant experience
- Instagram business profile
- Facebook page (now called "Events")

If you've been running video ad campaigns on Facebook, then you can select Video, which will pull up all the people who watched the video and then create a lookalike audience from them. Let's take a look at the video option.

The first thing that comes up is "Engagement". What this is about is how engaged were the people with your video. You can select the number of seconds they actually watched or a percentage. You probably don't want to create a lookalike audience from people that watched your video for just 3 seconds and left. A better metric might be picking people that watched it at least 50% of the way through – that demonstrates they had some significant interest in your offer even if they didn't follow through all the way to a sale. If you have multiple videos then you'll have to select the particular video you want to use.

Second, you need to select "In the Past" which gives a time frame in the number of days back that you want to use. In other words, if someone watched the video in the last 90 days, put 90 in the box. The default is the past year so it opens with 365 days.

Then name your audience and create it. Depending on how much data you have, i.e. how many people have watched the video since you posted it – it can take a few minutes for Facebook to crunch the data. When it's done it will give you two options:

- Create an ad using the audience
- Expand the audience

You'll want to expand the audience. This is a new set of people that Facebook gathers that match the people that watched your video in as many characteristics as possible. This brings up a new screen where you can set your parameters. These are similar to those used with an uploaded data set. The first thing is to specify one or more locations to use to generate the audience.

Then, use the sliding bar to pick an audience size. For the United States, if you set the bar at 5, it creates an audience with 10.7 million people. The values on the sliding bar indicate percentages of the population for your selected location. You can select a percentage between 1% and 10%.

Now you can save the audience, and it will be available when you create your next ad campaign. When you're in the audience section, use "Saved Audiences" to find and select it.

Page Likes

You can also use page likes to generate a lookalike audience. The steps are similar but let's quickly have a look. This time when you create your custom audience, select *Events*. Facebook will bring up a new screen which will ask you to select a Facebook page from the drop-down list (if you only have one page, that's what will be there). Make sure that you select People that have engaged from the drop-down list above the Facebook page, and then set the number of days that you want to use for the metric. From here on out, the instructions are the same.

74

The impact of the Lookalike audience

To get an understanding of what this is about let's roll back to advertising from scratch. To make it even worse, let's say you don't even do targeting. When you run your ad, Facebook is going to show it to everyone on Facebook (well, a small subset of them every day). As you might imagine most people aren't interested in your ad, so you get a lot of wasted impressions and wasted money.

As time goes on, the system optimizes, so it starts finding people that have an interest in your product, and then it can begin targeting others that are similar as it learns what their characteristics are. This, of course, can take some time to work right, and it's not going to go as well because Facebook doesn't have that much data at first.

Now let's consider what happens when you upload a Facebook audience. Suppose for the sake of an example that you're again targeting people that live in the Northeastern United States that want to move to Arizona. So far in our discussion of this type of ad, we have been talking about randomly finding them. What if instead, you were able to obtain a list of people that actually did move from the northeast to Phoenix.

These people are probably going to have a lot of surprising things in common. They may be a similar age, marital status, wealth, education level. Maybe most of them will come from a subset of occupations. Of course, most will be retired but we may still find out their occupation when they were still working. In addition, these people have been spending time on Facebook and leaving a trail of likes.

And so we buy a database of these people that have already moved from New York, Maine, Pennsylvania, Delaware, Connecticut, New Jersey, Rhode Island and Massachusetts to Arizona. We upload it to Facebook and then it cranks out an audience of millions of people who have the same characteristics. Including many of the same likes and so on in their Facebook history.

Now we can run ads targeting this new subset of people that Facebook has found for us. It won't be any surprise to learn that the ads that target these people are going to be far more effective than the ads that start cold. In fact, they are going to work like gangbusters!

Conversion rates are going to go through the roof. With that happening the cost to acquire new leads will plummet. You're going to have customers lining out the door wanting to buy a house in Phoenix from you (well provided it's in the right neighborhood).

As we said, lookalike audiences are the nuclear bomb of online advertising. Nobody else has anything as powerful as this.

CHAPTER 11
Creative Media Types

An ad campaign on Facebook has three vital elements that will help it drive traffic to your site or create page likes. These are the headline used for the ad, the text used in the ad, and the creative. As we've seen the creative can be a video, an image, a slide show, or what's called a carousel. Any type of creative can works as long as it's relevant and engaging. After all, a neutral photo is better than a bad video that drives people away. Let's take a look at the different creative types in more detail.

Single Image

This is the simplest kind of ad. Depending on what product or service that your offering, a single image can actually be quite relevant and engaging. For example, if you are selling t-shirts, you can have a picture of a nice looking young woman wearing the t-shirt in the image.

Facebook offers stock images that you can use if you are in a situation where you don't have anything you can use. These can still work too, although having your own creatives is a better path.

The ideal size for an image is a square that is 1080 x 1080. Remember that most people who are using Facebook are going to be doing it on a mobile device, so having a square image is better. If you don't have a square image, use the built-in cropping tools that Facebook has on the ad campaign creation page to make sure your image looks the way you want it to look when it displays on a mobile phone. You can use smaller images, but this is advertising – so you don't want to use something that might end up displaying with a blurry or pixelated appearance. If you don't have one of adequate size then you might want to simply use a stock image.

If you will be targeting your ads on Instagram as well as on Facebook, then you can use a different image for the Instagram ad. An Instagram ad is required to be at least 500 x 262 pixels in size.

Facebook allows you to create up to six ads using images for split testing. You can do this on the fly when you're creating the ad. Simply follow the instructions to upload or select all six images.

Video Creation Kit

For those who don't have any videos readily available, Facebook has introduced a very interesting option that research has shown is surprisingly effective. It's called Video Creation Kit and what it does is create a video from a series of still images and text that you enter. Video ads tend to have better conversion rates, so if you're looking at only being able to upload still images – you should strongly consider using the Video Creation Kit. As Facebook tells it, the tool lets you "create a Single video ad when you don't have a video".

There are two options that you can use for your template. You can opt to have a square video, or you can use a vertical template. Vertical videos are becoming a new rage since everyone is spending so much of their time on their mobile phones. In particular, if you are looking at advertising on Instagram then a vertical template might be of interest.

After you've decided whether to use square or vertical style template, there are options to choose between themes. Since the video creation kit is fairly new, there aren't very many options. But if Facebook decides to keep the video creation kit, we can expect that over time the options will be greatly expanded. Right now there are two general categories – Holiday and Standard. When you select the one you want, you'll see a small number of available templates.

For Standard, you'll see "Promote a Product", "Drive Product Delivery", and " Sell Multiple Products". How well these are tailored to their stated purpose is really hard to say, but they all produce nice flowing videos that come complete with interesting effects guaranteed to keep people's attention. The number of images used and video duration varies. These tend to be pretty short videos, which can be useful these days because so many people are developing short attention spans.

First, let's have a look at "Promote a Product". This option requires 2-5 images, and the video lasts 6 seconds. That is a flash in the pan – but for an advertisement to people with short attention spans it's probably a winner.

Next, we have "Drive Product Delivery". This one supposedly will "Inspire people to explore and shop by showing what makes your product unique". Playing around with the template I am not sure how it actually meets this fluffy goal – but it does make a nice video that can probably drive conversions. It requires 1-6 images and lasts 15 seconds.

Finally, there is "Sell Multiple Products" which has 4-7 images.

All three options make nice flowing video streams with some pretty cool effects. Especially if you are targeting a younger audience, you might consider these as potential tools even if you've got your own videos.

Slideshow

Facebook has other options if you're stuck with still images. One of these that comes to immediate use is an old-fashioned slideshow. This is an alternative to the video creation kit that can in a sense turn your ad created with still images into a "video". You can use 3-10 images to create the slideshow, which can last up to 15 seconds. Images that you use for the slideshow should have an aspect ratio of 16 x 9.

The slideshow will play in a loop when the ad is on the consumer's screen. Since you can include up to 10 images, you can include multiple marketing messages to help close the prospect.

Video

Now we arrive at the old gold standard- video. As YouTube is showing with its massive daily views, video remains at the top in the media world. You have more flexibility with video including putting up really long ads. For an advertisement that only runs on Facebook, a video can be up to 240 minutes in length. A video must be MP4 or MOV format and can be a maximum of 4 GB in size.

Whether you want to essentially distribute an ad that is a full-length movie or not, probably not, that gives you a lot of room to put together a video where you can deliver the entire message you want rather than trying to cram something into 6-15 seconds.

On Instagram, however, smaller attention spans dominate as people swipe here and there, so videos can only be 120 seconds long for Instagram feeds. Instagram has a second option which is to place video ads on "stories", but these can only be up to 60 seconds in length. Additionally, the stories are better served with vertical ads.

In-stream videos can be up to 15 seconds in length.

If you have a game or app that you're advertising on the audience network, the videos can be up to 120 seconds in length, and they must be at least five seconds. Games have so-called rewarded videos where people watch ads in exchange for in-game coins, these can only be 60 seconds in length.

So what is the ideal length for a video? Honestly, it depends on what you're selling. On television, we've seen both short and long. The standard 30-second ad seems to work pretty well, it keeps people's attention without going overboard. For most applications having a 30-second ad is probably ideal. Even then many are going to find it running too long and they'll probably not finish watching the entire video. However, something else we know about television is that people sit and watch infomercial ads that last a half-hour. So if it's appropriate, you can run a longer ad. However, in that scenario, you'll want to try and catch people at home. If someone is out, they probably aren't going to watch a 30-minute video even if they are somewhere that they have a connection. They may decide they'll watch it later, but most people will forget about it. You can minimize the damage by requiring a WiFi connection for your ad to be displayed. With this, you'll be able to catch a lot of people at home, when they are more likely to watch the entire ad and buy your product.

IMPORTANT: You're going to want to have a video with some screen time that has no text on the screen. Facebook has a silly rule that you can't have text displayed in the image used as the thumbnail for your video.

Instant Experience

On mobile devices, a new option is available called "instant experience". Although the experience is limited to the screen on the mobile device, Facebook claims it's "immersive". What this represents is an ad that fills up the entire screen when the user interacts with it. The ad can include all creative types – so you can include video, carousel, slideshow, and single images.

Carousel

This is an interesting ad creative type. You can think of this as a kind of upgrade from a slide show. You can mix together multiple media items into the same ad – and you can include both video and single images. However, while a slide show plays automatically through the different scenes, a carousel requires the user to move through them. So they have to swipe through each one, and view or not view videos that you have included.

You can even add a slideshow into the carousel.

Another interesting feature of carousels is each card (the individual part with an image or a video) can have its own headline and text. That way, you can convey multiple messages that might be relevant to your product or service. The default setting is to have three cards but you can add more.

Facebook will adjust the way the carousel works. As the ad runs, it will analyze the performance of each card you've added to the carousel. Then it will move the highest performing cards to the front end so that users will see them first.

Headlines and Text

Of course, writing your copy is a vital part of the ad. The headline is bold text and doesn't have much room to display, so keep your headlines simple. You will want to put your most compelling copy in the text. This isn't a copywriting course, but some suggestions are:

- Ask questions to get users engaged.
- Ask a type of question that might prompt an emotional response.
- Use phrases that imply some kind of secret is being revealed. For example, start off with "Discover the hidden method that...", "Previously hidden secret reveals...". It seems silly, but these kinds of phrases work at getting people engaged.
- After your initial question or phrase, list 2-3 benefits of your product or service.
- It can help to put a time limit "good for the next 72 hours".

CHAPTER 12
Boosted And Promoted Posts

If you're running a Facebook page, then you have the option to promote individual posts from the page. There are a couple of ways to get more eyeballs on posts, the first way is called "Boosted post", and you can also do "promoted" posts.

Boosted Posts

You can access posts from the Facebook Ads Manager drop-down menu. Open it up and select "All Tools". Then select "Page Posts". A new screen will open showing all your posts in a list. A boosted post doesn't have to be one that already exists, you can create a new one here. However, we'll look at boosting an existing post.

Select the post you want to "boost" by clicking on it in the list. It will open the post with a blue button in the lower right corner that says "Boost Post". Doing this is essentially creating an advertisement that is going to target the individual post you select. As such, you can do targeting on the screen that opens to boost the post, such as setting your audience in the same way when you create a normal ad campaign.

You're also going to see options for daily budget and automatic placements. Boosted Post campaigns have a fixed duration however, so you should set your duration after setting the other parameters. You can also set options for a website and pixel if you're going to use this to drive traffic (the pixel can help you track conversions).

If you decide to create a new post to boost, it's going to open up a screen where you set the ad campaign parameters.

You also have the ability to boost certain posts from your Facebook page. If you are on your Facebook page on the post stream, then you will see the Boost Post option there. Once you click on it, then the same steps are followed.

Promoted Posts

A promoted post is not too different, this time you create a new ad campaign using the Ads Manager. For this type of campaign, select Engagement. We did this earlier for page likes, this time select "Post engagement". Then you'll select all your options for the ad campaign just like any other, and the post that you want to promote.

CHAPTER 13
Common Mistakes Made By Newbies

Creating Facebook ads is a fairly simple exercise, but following the analytics and learning about all the options and more advanced features like the Facebook Pixel can be daunting. That means it's easy to make mistakes. In this chapter, we will look into some of the more common mistakes that people make when creating ad campaigns on Facebook.

Failing to set clear goals

If you're a veteran of advertising and marketing who's just new to Facebook, this won't be a problem for you. But one area where Facebook is catching fire is with small businesses that haven't done much advertising before. These might be very small businesses, someone with a Shopify account, doing digital product marketing or affiliate marketing, or someone doing Amazon FBA or even Kindle books. If you lack experience in marketing and advertising you might be tempted to just throw some ads up to see what happens and then hope that everything is going to work out in the end. Of course, you can't get through life and have success if you're not planning some things out and that applies here as much as it does anywhere else. In fact, it might be more important when it comes to advertising because you're throwing money out there.

So let's look at some basic goals or maybe we can call them parameters that you should set before launching your ad campaigns.

- Figure out the average lifetime value of your customers. If you don't know this yet, then estimate it. In short, you want to figure out the amount of stuff they are going to buy from you and get an average value. This is an important parameter for any business.
- Next, using the average lifetime value, you want to set an upper limit on the amount you can spend to acquire a customer. If you're going to have a billion customers, then

maybe you only want to make a penny in profit. But that isn't going to work for most of us. So get a comfortable margin, so that you can acquire enough customers and cover all your expenses while having some profit left over.

- Knowing the maximum cost of acquisition, now you have a solid benchmark for your ad campaigns. This will not be your goal specifically but will be the maximum cost per result that you will tolerate. Any campaign that fails to meet it must undergo adjustments to see if it can enter profitability quickly, and if it fails to deliver, shut off the campaign.
- Next, you need to know how many prospects you want to drive to your various media platforms. Don't run a page likes campaign and "see how it goes". Set a specific goal – maybe its 100 likes per day. Now you know the other side of the puzzle – how many campaigns and how many results you need to run in order to meet that goal.
- It goes without saying that you should know what your total budget can be! So figure out how much you can spend on advertising per month. Of course, Facebook is dynamic, so this is an upper limit. You may be able to optimize your Facebook campaigns to beat the budget.

Giving up too early

It's important to understand that the advertising network is dynamic. So you can't run your ad for a day and then think that is all there is going to be to the results. The longer you run your ad, the better the results are going to be.

Of course, in today's world, it's all about instant gratification. You can be forgiven if you get frustrated if results don't pour in during the first few hours of your ad campaign. Many people give up far too soon, without letting their campaigns run for an adequate time span and making important adjustments. One way that you can look at Facebook ads is that they are a simple kind of artificial intelligence. And a system that is built around artificial intelligence is one that needs time to learn. It learns fast but be sure to give it adequate time to learn. Generally speaking, 3-5 days is a time span you should shoot for when testing out ads to see if they are going to work for you. One area in particular where you might see massive improvement is the cost per result in your ad campaigns. On the first day, you might be getting a lot of results but they might cost more than expected. So give it time to work itself out. If by the third day you're still not seeing reductions in costs, then you'll need to go in and make basic adjustments. Look at everything – can the headline and text be improved? Is your video really a good creative that will compel people to click? Do you have interests, and demographics well targeted?

Setting Initial Budgets to High

A common mistake that many people make is taking Facebook at their word. When you set your budget, Facebook comes up with recommended values. Don't be naïve – you don't want to start out with the Daily Budget they recommend on a campaign that hasn't been tested at all. If you start out with a $40 daily budget on a completely untested brand new ad campaign – especially if you're a beginner and you don't have a lookalike audience – you might end up spending yourself into oblivion pretty quickly.

After having advertised on Facebook for many years, it's not really clear to me how and why they come up with the recommended budgets that they use. In all the years that I've advertised, I've never once settled on the recommended daily budget. Most of the time I have multiple campaigns running with budgets half the recommended amount or a few campaigns with much higher budgets.

The best approach is to start with a very low budget ($3-5) as we've discussed previously. Then follow the standard benchmark of raising it 15% per day until you've got it where you want it to be as far as quantity and cost per result.

Not Having Enough Ads

I like to watch the show Shark Tank, and there is a Canadian software billionaire named Kevin on there most of the time who everyone thinks is grouchy (they always call him Mr. Wonderful). The guy is actually a first-rate businessman and you should read his books and watch his YouTube videos. One of the pithy lessons he always uses is to let the market speak to you. Facebook lets this happen in real time and does in spades!

On Facebook, you can throw up lots of ads with lots of variations. The more ads that you put up simultaneously, the more data you're going to collect and the faster you're going to find out what works best for you. By putting up multiple ads that all vary in some way, you're going to find out what works to get you prospects while driving down your cost of acquisition a lot faster than you will if you're only running one or two ads and then trying to tweak them to get them to work. Put in all the tweaks ahead of time and then watch what happens. Then immediately kill all the ads that exceed your cost of acquisition for a customer. You are going to need to do this over a long enough time period so that you're not killing anything off prematurely, so as we've suggested before running the campaigns for at least three days, and preferably five days.

When you're just beginning, you might be overwhelmed creating twenty ads at once and then trying to keep track of them all. In that case, start off with five or ten ads. Remember we are shooting low, so they are going to have at most $5 budgets during the test phase.

And give them enough time. One time I was advertising an affiliate product on Facebook. At first, nothing happened. I ran the ad for a day and a half and nothing. What I am talking about here is nobody would even click to go to my website – much less drive a sale. I was about to kill the ad and then clicks started coming in on a regular basis. Every hour when I went to check the ad, I had gotten 5-10 more visits to my website. Moral of the story – make sure it runs at a minimum of three days.

Another thing that Kevin says in his lectures is that business is war. You may not like to think in those terms but it's a 100% accurate statement. Of course, nobody is going to show up and burn your house down and kill your family, but they are trying to destroy your business. In the war for customers, Facebook advertisers who are adapting quickly and getting their message out rapidly to most people are the winners. You do that by having more ads than your competitors. Information from the market is like intelligence on the battlefield – think of your multiple test ads as spies that are out in the field collecting intelligence so that your business can be on the winning side.

Not Using Lookalike Audiences

The first time that I heard about Lookalike audiences I have to admit I got a bit of a headache and my eyes glazed over. Back then, I didn't understand Facebook the way I do now, and I just wanted to run my ads without having to worry about all this complicated stuff. But once you learn how lookalike audiences work, your eyes get wide open. It's akin to a religious conversion.

Actually using a lookalike audience will blow you away. You're going to see unbelievable conversion rates and costs of acquisition that are well below your requirements. At the present time, in my opinion, the ability to use lookalike audiences makes Facebook the undisputed leader in advertising.

Lookalike audiences are so important, it might be a make or break situation when it comes to Facebook ads. If you can't find someone to share a lookalike audience with you or sell you one, then it is going to be worth the time, money and effort to build your own data so that you have enough to create a lookalike audience.

When you take that approach, you set up a feedback loop of success. The first time around that you run your ads, Facebook will be really struggling and it may be slow to bring you the number of customers you want at a price that is acceptable. But it gets better over time. After you've assembled enough likes or video views or whatever you choose as your input for the lookalike audience, then you feed them to Facebook and it's going to develop a super audience for you that will convert like crazy in comparison to your original campaigns. There is no way that you can consider running your business on Facebook without having tried lookalike audiences. Go after those stellar conversion rates and low cost of results.

Not Doing Research

Research for your Facebook campaigns isn't going to start when you are creating ad campaigns. You need to do it before you get to that point. And you don't need to be relying 100% on Facebook either. If you can find out information about the kind of people that are interested in the product or service that you offer, and find it outside of Facebook, that is just as useful. Then when you come to Audience Insights which is going to be your primary research tool on Facebook, you'll have some inputs to start with that will make your research that much more effective.

Then when you get on Audience Insights you need to drill down on all the things we've talked about. That includes knowing what pages they've liked, and actually taking the time to go and look through those pages and the websites of the companies that made the page. You'll also need to know where they live, what their job is, and so on. Of course, you'll need to know basic demographics like age and gender.

Not Keeping Up Your Facebook Page

I've stressed this time and again throughout the book – you need to keep your Facebook page active. In the old days, when it became clear that you needed content to keep Google happy and customers interested, people were able to get by creating a "content website" that had 10-20 pages of text-based around important SEO keywords. Then you could leave the site alone and the SEO would pull in organic traffic. Of course, you could advertise too, but if you were not a blogger you didn't worry very much about adding new content.

Well, that strategy still can work. But it's not going to work on Facebook. The reason is it's an interactive platform. You need to be engaged. That means putting up regular posts on your Facebook page that will keep your prospects coming back for more, and sharing more material with their friends. The more sharing the better. Also if you're posting frequently, it won't seem like spam the time you send everyone a note saying "check out my book, it's only $27". But if you do that after never adding a new post since they liked your page, you'll lose a lot of your newfound Facebook friends.

Also, remember that everything works two ways. We talked earlier about how you can use blogs and YouTube to push content to the

Facebook page. Facebook is a heavily trafficked site, so that means the converse can work for you-you can utilize the page to drive traffic to your blog or YouTube channel.

Also, look into the steps you can use to link your YouTube channel directly into your Facebook page. That way people can check out all your videos without having to leave Facebook.

Lack of a Strategy

Would you want to go into a war with a set of tactics, or a long term strategy with a clear winning goal in mind with an exit strategy? What about a football game? Is the best way to win a football game saying "pass a lot" or should you have a set of plays and a specific plan to deal with the opposing team? It seems to us that a strategy is better than just having a few tactics, even though tactics are important too.

Just tossing up Facebook ads and hoping for the best is a tactic. There is a chance that it will deliver results since Facebook is a great marketplace that lets you laser target your prospects. But doing that without an overall strategy isn't going to maximize your results. As we stated earlier before you launch your advertising campaigns you need to clearly lay out your goals and have a solid budget.

Ignoring Details

This book can't cover everything in the space allotted, so it's up to you to familiarize yourself with all the details in the Ads Manager. Ignoring some of the details can cost you unnecessary money that you don't need to spend. For example, on some of my mobile game campaigns, I began noticing that during the day downloads dropped a lot. The fact is that despite all the hype about people being addicted to their phones, they don't have time to download and play games during the middle of the day when they are busy at work. So would it make sense to be running my ads 24/7? Or should I run my ads when people are most likely to download them?

After you've run your campaigns for a few weeks, you'll need to take a deep dive into your data and ask yourself questions like these so that you can optimize campaigns. Too many beginners ignore all the details that Facebook makes available for them, and as a result, they fail to fully optimize their campaigns.

Being Afraid of Shutting Down Campaigns that Don't Deliver

We all get attached to things, even Facebook ads. If they are failing some people are going to have trouble letting go. It might seem like a personal failure when an ad you were sure would work failed to catch on. But this is business, and you shouldn't let emotions get in the way. Use a scientific approach and stick to the rules we've outlined for ending campaigns. Also keep in mind that times change, so you might develop some ads that run on all cylinders but then stop working all the time. Don't get attached to them and shut them down if they stop costing you money. There is no sense going down with a sinking ship.

Set Your Cost Targets

You need to know your marketing inside and out. That means knowing your cost per 1,000 impressions, and cost per click beside the cost per result. You need to be able to look at your campaigns in multiple ways to get a clear idea of what works and what doesn't.

Adapt to the ever-changing world of tech

Tech changes fast. It's easy to get lulled into sleep when something is working for you. We touched on that a little bit when we discussed the changes that web marketing went through when Google started paying attention to what was on people's websites. The thing about that situation is, that was not a one-time change. The technology companies are constantly changing how their algorithms work, or their terms of service. So it's important for you to keep up with what's going on and not fall asleep at the wheel.

Ad campaigns that you create this year may not be working in six months, because of some policy change that Facebook implements or changes in their algorithms. Spend time reading all their documentation, so you'll get wind of when things are changing or if they've altered their terms of service so that you can quickly move to make the changes you need to make.

Those who adapt to changes when they hit will be successful over the long term. It's no different than any other time in business, but the pace has accelerated. Those who fail to adapt will find themselves in a world of hurt that could be fatal to their business. It's even possible that at some point Facebook itself will become useless.

Getting the Right Placements

When you're just starting out, it's easy to not bother learning how things work under the hood and just accepting what Facebook gives you. That's true with Daily budgets and it's also true with placements. Facebook wants you to advertise far and wide, but that may not be in your best interests. So when they suggest automatic placements, you need to look into it first. Now keep in mind automatic placements may work for some people – but they may not work for others.

Placements can be important in determining what turns out to be a successful campaign and what doesn't. For various reasons, not all campaigns are suitable for running on all placements that Facebook offers. We've outlined a little bit about placements, for example, we talked about the relative skewing toward younger demographics on Instagram. That may help you or it may hurt you – but don't advertise on Instagram just because the system recommends it. If that is not your demographic, then don't waste time trying to get traffic there.

Far too many beginners simply go with Automatic placements when creating their ad campaigns. Don't make that mistake.

Using the Same Creatives

We've discussed this in other contexts. You should try running ads using different creatives. If possible, make multiple videos that you can test against one another. You can also test videos against slideshows or ads made with the video kit based on your static images. Then go with what works the best. If you follow major media on television, notice how they are constantly switching up ad content. Ads run for a while and then become stale.

Your ads are going to become stale too. So if you hit on a video that is really converting well, instead of relaxing by the pool you should be hard at work on your next video. Now a major media ad buy is going to show to the entire country over the course of a couple of months – you're reaching out to a far smaller subset of buyers on a daily basis. So your ads are not going to wear out as fast. However, you don't want to wait until they are done to start working on a replacement. Change out your videos or ad copy before your ads start declining or at least soon thereafter.

Not using Facebook Pixel

If you want to make people's eyes glaze over at a party, don't talk about physics, talk about computer coding. While the small band of devotees who are computer programmers love what they do, most people in the world are put off by computer code. In reality, it's a small thing, but when you start talking about the Facebook pixel people get put off. Maybe that's you too. But it's important to overcome your fear of the pixel. If it's too much for you, don't be embarrassed to seek out help. A developer will be happy to properly install it on your website. The Facebook pixel is one more tool in the Facebook arsenal and gives your marketing and advertising campaigns a power punch. Not using it is actually going to cost you money. In today's world information is power and the Facebook pixel is going to provide your business with large amounts of analytical information.

Failing to keep up with new technologies that Facebook may acquire

The acquisition of Instagram was a large move by Facebook. It's entirely possible that more acquisitions of that type will be made in the future. To have long term success, you should keep up with technology news and know what Facebook is doing. That way you won't be caught off guard when a new advertising platform shows up in placements.

The Seat of the Pants Approach

Many of the problems and mistakes we've been talking about actually belong in one category. Taking a seat of the pants approach to your business. Failing to set proper goals, failing to keep up with the changes at Facebook or the underlying technologies all add up to things that will keep your business from reaching its true potential.

CHAPTER 14
Facebook Business Manager

When starting out, you probably won't need it, but at some point, the Facebook Business manager will become important. In particular, if you're going to be using data for lookalike audiences obtained from outside sources, then you're going to need to migrate your ad account to Facebook business manager. The good news is that it's easy to do in a couple of steps and it doesn't cost you any money.

So what is it?

Facebook business manager arose out of the issue of Facebook users who were doing business activity being tied to a personal account. What Business Manager does is allow you to organize everything from your business activities in one central location. Some of the things that you can manage with the Facebook Business Manager include:

- Multiple ad accounts
- Facebook pages
- Multiple Facebook pixels
- Catalogs

It allows you to have this integration without sharing any of this information with your friends and coworkers. An issue that comes up is with business activities you may grow and need outside people to work with your Facebook ads account. Maybe they are developers that will need to access your Facebook pixel. Or maybe when you begin to grow you will hire someone to manage your Facebook pages or ad campaigns. You would probably like to do this without connecting them to your personal Facebook account. The Business Manager helps you do that.

When you set up the Facebook Business Manager, you will be able to invite others to your Facebook account to work on various aspects. Facebook has a routine signup process where you can enter basic information about your business. Once you sign up for

Facebook Business Manager, the first thing that you'll want to do is add an account. You can invite people using the following roles:

- Employee access
- Admin access
- Finance analyst
- Finance editor

Chances are, of course, that you are going to be the one who has the role of admin access. When you add employees, they can see all the business info but can only work on tasks that you assign to them.

Another aspect of Facebook Business Manager is having a central location where you can manage multiple Facebook pages and profiles without having to switch between them. Pages can be assigned to different people with roles in your company if desired.

You can also add Facebook Ad Accounts to the Business Manager (so you can have more than one ad account).

Now let's say that you have not enrolled in Facebook Business Manager. There are some actions you can take in the course of running your advertising operation that may trigger a situation where you are required to join. One example of this is the use of an external data source of customers with LTV (long term value) that you are uploading for the purposes of creating a lookalike audience. If you upload this data it will automatically take you to create your Facebook Business Manager enrollment. The process is very quick and easy, taking only a minute.

If you have a product catalog, you can upload it to Facebook Business Manager. A catalog is a database that has information about all the products in your inventory (if you have any). Once you've uploaded the catalog, then its available throughout the entire Facebook platform, such as on Instagram.

The Business Manager also provides a centralized location where you can manage Facebook Pixels for use in your advertising campaigns.

The Facebook Business Manager solves a lot of problems that Facebook used to have because of the ties to personal accounts. Now with Facebook Business Manager, you can have an overarching Business portal associated with Facebook where you can manage all your assets associated with Facebook including your Facebook Ad accounts, Facebook Pages, Facebook Pixels, a Catalog if you have one, and also manage people that will be working on your business. You can create employees and have employees or contractors work on various limited aspects of your business operations such as managing Facebook Pixels or one or more Facebook Pages.

CONCLUSION

Thank you for taking the time to read this book! We hope that you've found it enjoyable and informative.

The first lesson we'd like you to take away from this book is that you've learned how powerful Facebook really is as an advertising platform. Second, you should be ready to utilize all of the tools that Facebook has made available so that you can run the most successful ad campaigns. That includes being familiar with audience insights and using it to the fullest extent possible to know who your prospects are and what they are interested in. How many times have you heard in marketing that you need to have a vision of your typical customer inside your head? Now you don't need to guess – Facebook can tell you who your typical customer is, down to the last detail. You also need to take our comments about lookalike audiences to heart. Having used lookalike audiences in real Facebook ad campaigns, I'm fully aware of their power and how they can act like a rocket in driving your business results. It can't be said enough that failing to understand and utilize lookalike audiences might be one of the top mistakes when it comes to Facebook advertising. Leaving lookalike audiences on the table is akin to leaving a pile of cash on the table. Sure you might get by without it, but you'd be a lot better off using the power that it provides.

The second thing we hope that you'll take away from this book is to go into action with a plan. Start by knowing two key facts about your business: how much it costs to get a customer and how much money you're going to make from that customer. Those are the two most important numbers that you'll ever know. Once you know those two numbers, you can accurately map out a marketing and advertising strategy and budget. Second, you'll be able to accurately forecast your growth potential and be able to meet targets by realistically increasing your ad budget with time.

The third key ingredient to success is to test, test, and test. Remember to start out with small budgets and test multiple variations against each other in real time. If you can run 30 $5 per day ad campaigns at the same time – do it and find out which ones work. Don't be afraid to flush any campaigns that fail to deliver the results you need. Change up your images, videos, headlines, and ad copy as needed and revisit your demographics and interests if things aren't working out.

Finally, we want to wish you the best of luck in your Facebook ad campaigns, and we hope that the advice we have provided in this book will help you grow your business in ways you've never dreamed of. To your success! Again, if you've found this book interesting, useful, and informative, please be sure to leave a review. Thanks for reading!

www.ingramcontent.com/pod-product-compliance
Lightning Source LLC
Chambersburg PA
CBHW071722210326
41597CB00017B/2557